The Blooming of a Lotus

ESSENTIAL
GUIDED MEDITATIONS
FOR MINDFULNESS, HEALING,
AND TRANSFORMATION

Revised and Expanded Edition

Thich Nhat Hanh

Translated by Annabel Laity

BEACON PRESS · BOSTON

Beacon Press books
are published under the auspices of
the Unitarian Universalist Association of Congregations.

27 26 25 24   8 7 6 5 4 3 2 1

This book is printed on acid-free paper that meets the uncoated paper
ANSI/NISO specifications for permanence as revised in 1992.

Text design by Michael Starkman at
Wilsted & Taylor Publishing Services

Library of Congress Cataloging-in-Publication Data

Names: Nhat Hanh, Thích, author. | Laity, Annabel, translator.
Title: The blooming of a lotus : the essential guided meditations for
    mindfulness, healing, and transformation / Thich Nhat Hanh ;
    translated by Annabel Laity.
Description: Revised and expanded edition. | Boston : Beacon Press, [2022] |
    Summary: "In this revised edition of The Blooming of a Lotus, one of
    the world's great meditation teachers offers an expanded collection of
    exercises for practicing mindfulness meditation that will bring both
    beginning and experienced practitioners into closer touch with their
    bodies, their inner selves, their families, and the world"—Provided by
    publisher.
Identifiers: LCCN 2021045078 | ISBN 9780807020562 (paperback : acid-
    free paper) | ISBN 9780807017890 (ebook)
Subjects: LCSH: Meditation—Buddhism.
Classification: LCC BQ5612 .N47 2022 | DDC 294.3/4435—dc23
LC record available at https://lccn.loc.gov/2021045078

TABLE OF CONTENTS

PREFACE *v*

INTRODUCTION *ix*

Chapter One   Mindfulness of the Body *1*

Chapter Two   Feelings and Mental Formations *39*

Chapter Three   The Objects of Mind *75*

Chapter Four   Prefaces to Guide Meditation *127*

Chapter Five   Touching the Earth *151*

APPENDIX Ceremony
for Reciting the Five
Mindfulness Trainings *173*

RESOURCES *181*

PREFACE

In the Buddhist tradition, meditation transforms and heals. It helps us focus our attention so we become whole again, refreshed and stable. We learn to look deeply into ourselves and around us in order to realize what is really there. This insight helps us overcome our suffering and attachments. As we become more peaceful, happy, and free, we will no longer make ourselves or others suffer by the way we behave and speak. We will begin to transform our surroundings and to help others become more at ease, peaceful, and happy.

In order to be able to look and listen deeply, we need to restore our wholeness, to refresh, stabilize, and focus ourselves. To do this, we use the energy of mindfulness. Mindfulness is the state of being aware of what is happening in us and around us. Mindfulness shines light on the object of our meditation. That object could be a perception, an emotion, an action, or a reaction. It could be a physiological or a psychological phenomenon. Mindfulness helps us to look at and understand more deeply the nature and the origin of the object of our meditation.

While meditating, we constantly give rise to, nourish, and develop mindfulness. Mindfulness puts us in touch with life and everything that is happening in the present moment. Thus we live, look, and listen much more deeply. The result of looking and listening deeply is insight, awakening, and liberation.

As we meditate, we untie knots we have created in ourselves; knots of fear, hatred, anger, suspicion, despair, and attachment. A transformation takes place, gradually removing divisions and making our relationships with humans and nature much easier. We feel at ease and touch the joy of being alive, like a flower that is slowly opening. The human being is a species of flower that can bloom as freshly and beautifully as any other flower. The Buddha was a fully opened human flower, infinitely fresh and beautiful.

All of us are buddhas to be. That is why when people meet each other in a practice center, they form a lotus with their palms and greet each other, bowing and saying: "A lotus for you, a buddha to be." Breathing in, saying "a lotus for you," and breathing out, smiling, saying "a buddha to be," they embody the freshness of a blooming flower.

In the Buddhist tradition, the sangha is seen as a precious jewel. There are three precious jewels: Buddha, Dharma, and sangha. These three jewels are already in your heart. They will guide you to the sangha that is somewhere near you.

If you have not yet found a good teacher or a sangha, you can still practice alone. A good teacher is someone who has experienced and realized the fruits of practice. A sangha is a community where everyone follows more or less the same kind of practice. Since everyone is doing the same practice, it becomes easier for you to practice, too, because the group energy emitted by the sangha is strong and supportive. You can also learn a great deal from individual members of the sangha, especially those who have realized some degree of peace and transformation. There are many things you may find difficult to do when alone, but in the presence of the sangha, you can do them easily. Those of us who have practiced with a sangha can testify to this fact.

If you have not yet had the chance to encounter a teacher and a sangha, this book can help you in the beginning. All the guided meditations in this book have been taken from the basic dhyana sutras of Source Buddhism[1] and Mahayana Buddhism. They have been taught by the Buddha and enlightened teachers and sanghas

---

1. We have used the term "Source Buddhism" to describe the earliest phase of Buddhism, belonging to the lifetime of Buddha Shakyamuni.

throughout the history of Buddhism. Before being published in this book, these meditations have been regularly practiced at the Plum Village Monastery in France, and during the many retreats led by Thich Nhat Hanh over the years, often being adapted to respond to the prevailing needs of the world. Therefore, the book you hold is the fruit of the experience and practice of the teacher and also of the students.

As you practice the exercises, you will feel the support of good teachers and the sangha.

When you have practiced some of these guided meditations for a while, you will generate for yourself the energy of mindfulness. You will feel refreshed, more focused, and happier. There may be that sangha is very close to where you live, but you have not been in touch with them yet.[2] Please have trust and start to practice the meditations right away.

Everything depends on your practice of mindfulness. You are a flower that could bloom at any time, a future buddha. We wish you good luck.

2. Find your sangha with the Plum Village interactive map: https://plumvillage.org/about/international-sangha-directory.

INTRODUCTION

How to Use This Book

Meditation can be practiced almost anywhere—while sitting, walking, lying down, standing; even while working, eating, and using the toilet. The exercises in this book are principally used to guide and strengthen one's practice of sitting meditation.

For more than thirty years, many thousands of people have come to Plum Village to practice meditation. Many of them find sitting meditation most effective. Others have more success with walking meditation, tea meditation, or mindful service. Ultimately, everyone who has attended retreats in Plum Village has benefited from these exercises.

At first, those who are used to sitting silently to meditate do not feel at ease during the guided meditation; they may even feel irritated. But with practice, they are able to experience its many benefits and consequently experience transformation at a very fundamental level. Over the years, meditation students from many parts of the world have asked me to make these exercises more widely available.

THE SUBJECT MATTER OF THE GUIDED MEDITATION

The guided meditations in this book have different purposes. Some exercises are done simply to nourish the joy of being alive. Others help us be in touch with life, help us heal, look deeply, or let go. Some exercises combine two or three of these functions at the same time.

Usually, the exercises that nourish our body and mind are used to guide us at the beginning of a retreat. These exercises can be called the food of joy. In the Dhyana School, there is the expression "meditation as the food of joy," which means that the feeling of joy arising from the practice of meditation nourishes and sustains us. During the ceremony for offering rice at midday, we say, "Receiving this food, we pray that everyone will be nourished by the enjoyment of the meditation practice and the enjoyment of the Dharma that will bring them to the realization of the full truth."

The first part of this book contains this kind of meditation. The exercises connect us to elements that are refreshing and healthy, both in ourselves and in the world around us. They help us put an end to distracted thoughts and bring us back to the present moment, where we can recognize the oneness of body and mind. Although they are called nourishment exercises, they also restore internal balance, allowing the body as well as the mind to begin the work of healing. Some of these meditations help us renew contact not only with our self, our body, and our mind, but also with the world at large, with family, and with society. We thus learn to overcome blockages, loneliness, and isolation, and a way of transformation and healing opens up before us.

Another function of meditation is looking deeply. You use insight to light up the recesses of your mind or to look into the heart of how things are. Whether the object is psychological or physical, you begin to see its true nature so you are no longer driven or oppressed by it. In this process, you develop an insight called *prajña*. This insight can heal and help us let go of what is driving us. Some of the meditations on looking deeply are to heal us, others to help us let go, and some even have both these functions.

The person who guides the meditation session needs to choose the meditation that fits the needs of the practitioners, just as a doctor will prescribe the medicine appropriate for the patient.

Practitioners can judge from experience which exercises are most suitable for their needs and the circumstances in which they find themselves. Some meditations are to be practiced in the beginning, others later on, and some need us to wait until our practice is more solid.

THE BEST WAY TO GUIDE MEDITATION

Those who are chosen to guide sitting meditation exercises should be experienced in the practice of meditation; that is, they themselves should have realized an inner transformation. They should know how to invite the bell during the meditation in a firm and unhurried way, so that the sound of the bell expresses and gives rise to a stable and calm state of mind. The voice of the guide should be neither too loud nor too soft. It should inspire and at the same time soothe. The guide must be sensitive to the needs and the health of the participants. The subject matter of the guided meditation and the length of time allotted to it will be based on this understanding. If the participants experience joy, well-being, and other benefits as a result of the session of guided meditation, then the guide can be said to have succeeded in the task.

In this book, you will find explanatory notes following each exercise. These explanations are to help you understand the purpose of the meditation. They are not to be read during the meditation session. If, after you have practiced the guided meditation, you want to have further understanding of its function, you can read the explanation.

The guided meditation session begins with three sounds of the bell or the meditation chant.[1]

After that, enough time is allowed for the sound of the bell to die away and the person guiding the meditation wakes the bell up. This is done by placing the baton firmly against the rim of the bell

---

1. See Thich Nhat Hanh, *Chanting from the Heart: Buddhist Ceremonies and Daily Practices* (Berkeley, CA: Parallax Press, 2006).

and not moving it away immediately. This produces a muffled sound that will attract the attention of the hearers without startling them. Then, after one slow in-breath and out-breath, the guide enounces clearly the first sentence of the exercise: one line for the in-breath and one for the out-breath. Any guided meditation should begin with a reminder for the practitioners to return to their breathing in order to calm the body and mind. For example:

> *Breathing in, I am aware of my in-breath*
> *Breathing out I am aware of my out-breath.*

Following this, the guide says the key words for these two lines:

> *In-breath, out-breath.*

The key words restate the main intent of the two preceding lines and help the practitioners concentrate on them. After the key words, there is a full (unmuffled) sound of the bell.

Now allow at least ten and possibly twenty or more full in- and out-breaths to elapse in silence for the practitioners to practice deeply and with stability this stage of the meditation. After this interlude, invite again the muffled sound of the bell before enouncing the words of the next two lines with their key words. They will again be succeeded by a full sound of the bell, a silent period, and so on until the end of the exercise.

In many exercises, the in-breath may be accompanied by an image and the out-breath with another image, based on the preceding one. Using an image to meditate on is much easier and more useful than using an abstract idea. The image accompanies the breath, and the mindful breathing helps carry the image into our consciousness. For example, exercise 1 of chapter 2:

> *Breathing in, I see myself as a flower.*
> *Breathing out, I feel fresh.*
> *Flower, fresh.*

The voice of the guide should be expressive of the spirit and the image upon which the participants are concentrating.

Sometimes a guided meditation has several parts that can be practiced over several periods of meditation.

After a session of guided practice, the person leading the meditation should be ready to hear the reactions of the participants, so that in the succeeding sessions, the meditation can better fit their needs. This requires a little practice, and we should train ourselves to guide meditation so that at some time in the future we can help others.

BREATHING AND LOOKING DEEPLY

Mindful breathing is a basic meditation practice. Very few people can be truly successful in the art of meditation without the help of mindful breathing. To practice conscious breathing is to open the door to stopping and looking deeply in order to enter the domain of concentration and insight. The meditation master Tang Hoi, the first patriarch of the Dhyana School in Vietnam (third century CE), said that "Anapananusmriti [being aware of breathing] is the great vehicle offered by the Buddhas to living beings" (from the preface to the Anapananusmriti Sutra).[2] Conscious breathing is the way into the four meditative concentrations[3] and all other kinds of samadhi (concentration). Conscious breathing also leads us into the basic insights of impermanence, emptiness, interdependent origination, selflessness, and nonduality in all that is. It is true that we can practice stopping and looking deeply without using conscious breathing, but conscious breathing is the safest and surest path we can follow. Thus, all the exercises presented here employ the vehicle of conscious breathing. The breathing is like a vehicle conveying the image, and the image breaks through the mists of our wrong perceptions.

2. Thich Nhat Hanh, *Master Tang Hoi: First Zen Teacher in Vietnam and China* (Berkeley, CA: Parallax Press, 2001), v.

3. Thich Nhat Hanh, *The Heart of the Buddha's Teaching: Transforming Suffering into Peace, Joy & Liberation* (Berkeley, CA: Parallax Press, 1998), v.

MEDITATING ON YOUR OWN

It goes without saying that it is preferable to practice meditation under the guidance of a teacher and in the company of good spiritual friends, from whom you receive energy and support. You can learn a great deal not only from the experience of your teacher but also from your friends, especially those who have inner peace and happiness and know how to transform their difficulties. The meditations in this book can be used to guide a community of practitioners or a group of friends, as well as for someone practicing alone. You can also practice alone and with a group, and your personal practice will complement the practice you do with the group.

Even if you do not have a sangha and have to practice alone, you can rest assured that the meditations in this book will help you transform your life and lessen your suffering. There is no danger of going astray if you practice these meditations on your own, although if you want to do other meditation practices, such as congan[4] practice, you should do so only under the guidance of a good teacher. The guided meditations in this book are original Buddhism as taught by the Buddha. You can put them into practice as soon as you have read them without having to wait for a teacher, and it is quite possible that later on, you will find your teacher or your sangha.

"YOU ONLY NEED TO SIT."

Some of us do not know what we should be doing during sitting meditation. We have been taught a correct meditation posture, for example, how to sit with both knees on the ground and imagining that the crown of our head is being pulled up by a string towards the sky. We could sit like that for months or years without know-

---

4. *Congan* means your teacher entrusts you with the object that is most suited to your needs for you to concentrate on day and night.

ing how to calm our breathing and bring body and mind together as one. We could be sitting as if in a dark cave. At the very least, the meditations in this book let us know what we could be doing as we sit in meditation.

Your sitting posture should be as comfortable as possible. Relax every muscle in your body, including the muscles of your face. The best way to relax the muscles of your face is to smile gently and maintain the smile throughout the meditation. Keep your spinal column quite straight, but not rigid. In this comfortable position, you can feel well during the whole time of sitting. Do not make too much effort and do not struggle. Let go of everything and you will not cause yourself backache, shoulder-ache, or headache. If you are able to find a cushion that fits your body well, you can sit for a long time without feeling tired.

"You only need to sit" is an exhortation of Tao Dong (Soto) meditation school. It means that you should sit without waiting for a miracle—and that includes the miracle of enlightenment. If you sit in expectation of something, you cannot be in touch with or enjoy the present moment, where life and everything else is available. *To sit* here means really to sit, mindful, at ease, calm, peaceful, happy, and clear. Only this kind of sitting is beneficial. It takes training and practice. It is not enough to obey the order: *"just sit."* *"You only need to sit"* only has meaning when you sit mindfully, peacefully, and happily.

SOME RESISTANCES TO GUIDED MEDITATION

Some people find the sound of the bell and the spoken voice during the sitting meditation session disturbing. Accustomed to silence while meditating, they feel that their peace and joy is taken away from them in guided meditation. This is not difficult to understand. In silent meditation, they have been able to calm their body and mind. Obviously while in such a state, they do not want to be disturbed. But, if they feel satisfied by this state of calm, they will not be able to go far in the work of transforming the internal knots that lie in the depths of their consciousness. There are people who meditate only to forget the complications and problems of life, like rabbits crouching under a hedge to escape a hunter, or people taking shelter in a cellar to avoid bombs. The feeling of security and protection arises naturally when people sit in meditation, but they cannot continue in this state forever. On the contrary, we need meditation to make us strong and healthy so we can return to daily life and help be an agent of change in society.

Practicing guided meditation, we have the opportunity to be in touch with the wonders of life in our selves that nourish us and bring us more peace and joy. In addition, we can look deeply into our minds to sow and cultivate there the wholesome seeds that are able to transform suffering. Finally, we are guided to face and be present for that suffering in order to understand its roots and be free of its bondage.

Guided meditation is not some new invention. It was used by practitioners in the time of the Buddha. This is clear if you read the Sutra for the Sick and the Dying (Ekottara Agama, chapter 51, sutra 8; Madhyama Agama, sutra 26; or Majjhima Nikaya, sutta 143). This sutra records the guided meditation that Sariputra used to help the layman Anathapindika when he was lying on his sick bed. The Venerable Sariputra guided Anathapindika step by step until he was able to transform his fear of death. The Anapanasati Sutta is also a guided meditation teaching. In short, guided meditation has been part of the Buddhist tradition right from the beginning. There is no need to feel resistance to it.

The guided meditation exercises in this book can help many practitioners by making their sitting meditation more concrete. So far in the history of Buddhist meditation, there has never been a book guiding us systematically in how to meditate. This systemization could open a new era for the practice of sitting meditation.

BREATHING WITH SONG AND MUSIC

Before a Dharma talk, a Dharma sharing, or a session of Beginning Anew, the community or group of friends can breathe to the sound of a song or music. There are a number of meditation exercises that have been put to music, for example: *"In, out, deep, slow"* or *"Breathing in, breathing out, I am blooming as a flower."* These songs help us remember the words of the guided meditation. Once a meditation is memorized, it is much easier to put it into practice in a natural way, whether you are sitting or engaged in an activity.

While singing, you practice the words you are singing. If you sing the word "flower," you feel the freshness of the flower as you sing. You can also use the singing or music of the song as an accompaniment to your breathing. One half of the group can sing as the other half listens and breathes, and then the two halves change roles.[5]

FURTHER RECOMMENDATIONS FROM
THICH NHAT HANH ON GUIDING MEDITATION

During the past twenty years, we have had the good fortune to be able to accompany Thich Nhat Hanh as he toured the world offering retreats. Often, we were designated by the sangha to offer guided meditations. Since Thich Nhat Hanh was always present in the sitting meditation sessions that began the day of practice, he often offered a critique on the way the meditation was led by the monks or nuns. Here follow some of his recommendations.

1. When practicing meditation, we should engage our whole being and not the intellect alone. When we guide meditation, it is important to engage the deeper levels of consciousness of those who are practicing, rather than the intellect. For this reason, we

---

5. For all songs, please refer to http://plumvillage.org/library/songs/.

do not begin the meditation session with instructions on how to meditate or explanations of the guided meditation that is about to follow. Such instructions necessarily over-engage the intellect of the practitioners. In large retreats for sometimes a thousand or more practitioners, instructions on how to find a correct sitting posture and how to follow the guided meditation are given in a separate orientation on the previous day. At the beginning of the meditation session, the powerful morning chant accompanied by the sound of the bell is sung by a monk or a nun.[5] After the chant, the guided meditation begins. If meditators have, for some reason, received no previous instructions, a simple reminder to keep the back straight and relaxed will suffice. If the morning chant is not offered, three sounds of the bell can begin the session.

2.   During a retreat, all participants should learn how to be aware of the breath in order to calm and relax their body. This is the most fundamental meditation practice. Therefore exercises 1, 2, 3, or 4 of chapter 1 should be offered during the first meditation session of every retreat. Every time a meditator practices according to these exercises, they will obtain some deepening of their practice. Each time we sit, our body and mind are in a different state, and our experience of the same guided meditation changes. We need not hesitate to offer these meditations at the beginning of every retreat, even though some of the retreatants present may already be familiar with them.

3.   After attending a retreat, all retreatants should know how to take care of their wounded child within and how to begin to reconcile with their parents. Exercise 7 of chapter 3 should be offered toward the end of the retreat. Enough time should be allotted to complete the whole exercise.

6. See appendix at the end of this book.

CHAPTER 1

Mindfulness
of the Body

*I*n the *Anapanasati Sutta*,[1] the Buddha teaches mindfulness
of breathing as a guided meditation. There are sixteen exercises
divided equally into four parts. The first part is using the breath to
be mindful of the body. The second is using the breath to be mindful of the feelings. The third is breathing to be mindful of the mind
and mental formations. The fourth is breathing to be mindful of
the objects of the mind. The Sutra on the Four Establishments of
Mindfulness (Satipatthana)[2] is another fundamental meditation
sutra that addresses these four fields of mindfulness (mindfulness
of the body, feelings, mental formations, and objects of mind). It
is learned by heart by monks and nuns in Myanmar (Burma) and
Thailand, and read to the dying by those who accompany them. In
The Blooming of a Lotus, all four of these areas or fields of mindfulness are covered. The exercises on mindfulness of the body are the
most basic practice and can be used at any time as an introduction to
exercises for looking deeply and transforming. They help us become
accustomed to breathing consciously and to use the breathing to

1. Thich Nhat Hanh, *Breathe, You Are Alive! The Sutra on the Full Awareness of
Breathing* (Berkeley, CA: Parallax Press, 1990).

2. Thich Nhat Hanh, *Transformation and Healing: Sutra on the Four Establishments
of Mindfulness* (Berkeley, CA: Parallax Press, 1990).

unite body and mind. The fourteen guided meditations of chapter 1
are based on the first four breathings of the Anapanasati Sutta and
the section of the Satipatthana Sutta on mindfulness of the body.

EXERCISE 1

Returning to My Body
in the Present Moment

1. Breathing in, I know I am breathing in.   *in*

   Breathing out, I know I am breathing out.   *out*

2. Breathing in, I am aware of the whole   *whole length*
   length of my in-breath.   *of in-breath*

   Breathing out, I am aware of the whole   *whole length*
   length of my out-breath.   *of out-breath*

3. Breathing in, I am aware of my whole   *my whole body*
   body.

   Breathing out, I relax my whole body.   *I relax*

4. Breathing in, I calm my body.   *Calming body*

   Breathing out, I smile.   *Smiling*

5. Breathing in, I dwell in the present   *present*
   moment.   *moment*

   Breathing out, it is a wonderful   *wonderful*
   moment.   *moment*

Many people begin to practice sitting meditation with the help of
this exercise. Even those who have meditated for many years continue to practice it, because it is so effective.

Breathing in, bring complete attention to the in-breath. Wherever the breath may be in the body, feel the calm it brings. Just like drinking cool water on a hot day, feel how the breath cools the inner organs of the body. When practicing meditation, if the body is calm, then the mind is calm. Conscious breathing makes the body and mind one. Breathing out, smile to relax all the facial muscles (the face has about forty small muscles in all). The nervous system will also become relaxed. The half-smile can be seen as the fruit of the calm brought by the in-breath, but it is also a means of relaxing your body and mind, and makes us more aware of our peace and joy.

This exercise brings you back to the present moment. By dwelling in the present moment, you put an end to attachments to the past and anxieties about the future. Life is only available in the present. It is necessary to return to this moment to be in touch with life as it really is. To be alive, and to touch all the wonders of life within you and around you, is truly a miracle. We need only to open our eyes and to listen carefully to enjoy life's richness. That is why the present moment can be the most beautiful and wonderful moment when you know how to be aware of your breathing to bring yourself back.

This exercise can be practiced anywhere at any time: in the meditation hall, in the kitchen, on the bank of a river, in a park, on a train or bus, whether you are walking or standing still, lying down or sitting, even when you are working.

EXERCISE 2
Dwelling in the Present Moment

1. Breathing in, I know I am breathing in.   *in*

    Breathing out, I know I am breathing out.   *out*

2. Breathing in, my breath grows deeper.   *deep*

    Breathing out, my breath grows slower.   *slow*

3.	Breathing in, I calm my body.	*calm*
	Breathing out, I feel at ease.	*ease*
4.	Breathing in, I smile.	*smile*
	Breathing out, I release.	*release*
5.	Breathing in, I dwell in the present moment.	*present moment*
	Breathing out, it is a wonderful moment.	*wonderful moment*

This exercise can also be practiced anywhere, in the meditation hall, in the living room, in the kitchen, or while on a train.

The first stage is designed to bring body and mind back together, while at the same time helping us come back to the present moment and to connect us with the miracle of life. If we can breathe in this spirit for two or three minutes, our breathing will quite naturally become lighter, leisurely, gentler, slower, and deeper, and we shall feel much more at ease in body as well as in mind. The second stage is "deep, slow." We can stay with this stage for as long as we like.

Next we come to "calm, ease." Here we can achieve deeper tranquility (in Sanskrit, *prasrabdhis*), a great calming of body and mind, in which the joy of meditation will continue to nourish us. You can practice *"present moment, wonderful moment"* as you did in exercise 1 in order to feel the happiness of being right here and right now. This exercise has been put to music, and you can learn it by heart by singing it.[3]

3. For all songs, please refer to http://plumvillage.org/library/songs/.

EXERCISE 3

Smiling to Life

---

1. Breathing in, I am aware, this is an in-breath.   *in-breath*

    Breathing out, I am aware, this is an out-breath.   *out-breath*

2. Breathing in, my breath grows deeper.   *deep*

    Breathing out, my breath grows slower.   *slow*

3. Breathing in, I enjoy my in-breath.   *enjoy in-breath*

    Breathing out, I enjoy my out-breath.   *enjoy out-breath*

4. Breathing in, I have a body, it is alive, a wonder of life.   *I have a body*

    Breathing out, I smile to my body.   *I smile*

5. Breathing in, I smile to my body.   *smile*

    Breathing out, I release the tensions in my body.   *release tensions*

6. Breathing in, I know that I'm alive.   *alive*

    Breathing out, I smile to life within and around me.   *smiling to life*

7. Breathing in, I dwell in the present moment.   *present moment*

    Breathing out, it is a wonderful moment.   *wonderful moment*

EXERCISE 4

Joy of Meditation While Relaxing the Body

1. Breathing in, I know I am breathing in.   *in*

   Breathing out, I know I am breathing out.   *out*

2. Breathing in, my breath grows deep.   *deep*

   Breathing out, my breath goes slowly.   *slow*

3. Breathing in, I am aware of my body.   *my body*

   Breathing out, I relax my body.   *relax*

4. Breathing in, I calm my body.   *calm body*

   Breathing out, I care for my body.   *care for body*

5. Breathing in, I smile to my body.   *smile*

   Breathing out, I feel ease in my body.   *ease*

6. Breathing in, I smile to my body.   *smile*

   Breathing out, I release the tensions   *release*
   in my body.

7. Breathing in, I'm aware of my stable   *stable posture*
   posture.

   Breathing out, I enjoy the stability.   *I enjoy it*

8. Breathing in, I feel joy.   *joy*

   Breathing out, I enjoy peace and   *peace, happiness*
   happiness.

9. Breathing in, I dwell in the present   *present moment*
   moment.

   Breathing out, it is a wonderful moment.   *wonderful*
                                                moment

Although this exercise is easy and pleasant to practice, it is of immense benefit to all who practice it. Through this exercise, many people who are just beginning to meditate can taste the pure joy that meditation brings. Moreover, those who have already been practicing for some years can use this exercise to nourish body and mind and to continue further on the path of meditation.

The first stage (*in, out*) is to identify the breath. If this is an in-breath, the practitioner must be aware that it is an in-breath. If this is an out-breath, the practitioner must be aware that it is an out-breath. While concentrating on the breath even a few times, the practitioner will naturally stop thinking about the past and the future, putting an end to dispersed thoughts. This happens because the mind of the meditator is wholly with the breathing, in identifying the in-breath and the out-breath. In this way, the meditator has become one with the breathing. The mind is no longer an anxious mind or a thinking mind; it is simply a breathing mind.

The second stage (*deep, slow*) is to see that the in-breath is already growing deeper and the out-breath has already slowed down. This process happens of itself and does not require any effort on the part of the meditator. To breathe and to be aware that you are breathing (as in the first stage of the exercise) naturally makes the breathing deeper, slower, more even. In other words, the breathing has more quality. When the breathing has become even, calm, and rhythmic, the practitioner begins to feel peace and joy in body as well as in mind. The tranquility of the breathing brings about the tranquility of the body and mind. At this point, the meditator begins to experience meditation as the food of joy.

The third stage (*awareness of the whole body, relaxing the whole body*) brings the mind home to the body with the in-breath, and the mind becomes acquainted with the body. The breathing is the bridge that takes the meditator from the body to the mind and from the mind to the body. The function of the out-breath is to relax the whole body. While breathing out, the meditator allows the muscles in the shoulders, in the arms, and then in the whole body to relax so that a feeling of comfort is experienced in the whole body. This stage should be practiced for at least ten in- and out-breaths.

The fourth stage (*calming the body, caring for the body*) calms the functions of the body with the in-breath. With the out-breath, the meditator expresses a heartfelt compassion for the needs of the body. If the meditator continues to practice this fourth stage, the breath will be utterly calming and help the meditator to treat the body with deep respect and care.

The fifth stage (*smiling to the whole body, feeling ease in the body*) brings relaxation to all the facial muscles. The meditator sends the half-smile to the whole body, as if it were a fresh, cool stream of water. To ease the body is to feel well and relaxed. This stage of the exercise nourishes the whole body through the compassion of the meditator.

The sixth stage (*smiling to the body, releasing the tensions in the body*) is a continuation of the fifth stage. Here, the breathing helps dissipate all the tensions that still remain in the body.

The seventh stage (*stable posture, enjoying*) steadies the meditator in the sitting position he has adopted. It will help us be aware that our posture is not yet straight or solid, and then we can move to correct it. A stable sitting posture brings about ease and enjoyment of that stability. The meditator becomes master of their body and mind and is not pulled hither and thither by the different actions of body, speech, and mind, in which they might otherwise drown.

The eighth stage (*feeling joy, feeling happy*) brings awareness of the feeling of joy when the meditator breathes in. This is the joy of being alive, of having good health, of being able to nourish the body at the same time as the mind. The out-breath brings a feeling of happiness. To sit with nothing to do but to breathe mindfully is a great happiness. Countless people bounce around like yo-yos in their busy lives and never have the chance to feel this meditator's joy.

The ninth stage (*present moment, wonderful moment*) brings the meditator back to the present moment with the in-breath. The Buddha taught that the past has already gone and the future has not yet come; that we find life in what is happening now. To dwell in the present is truly to return to life. Only in the present moment is the meditator really in touch with the wonders of life. Peace, joy, liberation, the buddha nature, and nirvana cannot be found anywhere else. Happiness lies in the present moment. The in-breath helps the meditator be in touch with this happiness. The out-breath also brings much happiness to the meditator, and that is why he says "wonderful moment."

EXERCISE 5
In Deep Contact with the Parts of My Body

1. Breathing in, I am aware of the hair on my head.   *my hair*

   Breathing out, I smile to the hair on my head.   *I smile*

2. Breathing in, I am aware of my eyes.   *my eyes*

   Breathing out, I smile to my eyes.   *I smile*

3. Breathing in, I am aware of my ears.   *my ears*

   Breathing out, I smile to my ears.   *I smile*

4. Breathing in, I am aware of my teeth.   *my teeth*

   Breathing out, I smile to my teeth.   *I smile*

5. Breathing in, I am aware of my smile.   *my smile*

    Breathing out, I smile to my smile.   *I smile*

6. Breathing in, I am aware of my shoulders.   *my shoulders*

    Breathing out, I smile to my shoulders.   *I smile*

7. Breathing in, I am aware of my arms.   *my arms*

    Breathing out, I smile to my arms.   *I smile*

8. Breathing in, I am aware of my lungs.   *my lungs*

    Breathing out, I smile to my lungs.   *I smile*

9. Breathing in, I am aware of my heart.   *my heart*

    Breathing out, I smile to my heart.   *I smile*

10. Breathing in, I am aware of my liver.   *my liver*

    Breathing out, I smile to my liver.   *I smile*

11. Breathing in, I am aware of my bowels.   *bowels*

    Breathing out, I smile to my bowels.   *I smile*

12. Breathing in, I am aware of my kidneys.   *kidneys*

    Breathing out, I smile to my kidneys.   *I smile*

13. Breathing in, I am aware of my feet.   *my feet*

    Breathing out, I smile to my feet.   *I smile*

14. Breathing in, I am aware of my toes.   *my toes*

    Breathing out, I smile to my toes.   *I smile*

This exercise helps us be more deeply in contact with our body. The in-breath is to focus on a certain part of the body: eyes, ears, heart, lungs, and so on. The out-breath smiles to that part of the body. The half-smile can calm and heal. It expresses care and tenderness for the body. The lungs, the heart, and the liver work diligently over many decades, but how often do we take the time to show them any attention and compassion? Not only do we fail to recognize when these parts of the body are tired and out of sorts, but we frequently treat them in a brutal way, weakening them even further. The liver is destroyed by drinking alcohol. Incorrect breathing weakens the lungs, making them vulnerable to disease, and at the same time undermines the other organs of the body. If we are always anxious, worrying, or over-emotional, or if we eat too much fat, we can put our hearts at risk. But by breathing consciously and being in touch with all the different parts of the body, we come to feel and understand the body, and we learn in a concrete way how to bring it peace and joy. The peace and joy of the body is nothing other than our own peace and joy. This exercise is an exercise of loving meditation toward the body. If we are not able to love our own bodies, then how can we love anyone else?

The first time you practice this exercise, you might think that it is too simple, but after you have been practicing it for some time, you will see how important it is. At first you just recognize and smile to the different parts of your body, but gradually you will see each individual part very clearly and deeply. Every hair and every cell contains all the data necessary to make the universe. That is the teaching of interdependence found in the Avatamsaka Sutra. Every hair on your head is a message from the universe. You can realize awakening by meditating on a single strand.

If you are practicing on your own, you can use this exercise when you are lying down to relax or to go to sleep.

EXERCISE 6

Caring for Each Organ of My Body

1. Breathing in, I see myself as a five-year-old child.   *myself five years old*

   Breathing out, I smile to the five-year-old child.   *I smile*

2. Breathing in, I see myself at ninety years old.   *myself ninety years old*

   Breathing out, I smile to myself at ninety years old.   *I smile*

3. Breathing in, I see my body as it is now.   *my body now*

   Breathing out, I smile to my body as it is now.   *I smile*

4. Breathing in, I am aware of my face as it is now.   *my face now*

   Breathing out, I smile to my face as it is now.   *I smile*

5. Breathing in, I am aware of the state of my skin.   *state of skin*

   Breathing out, I smile to the state of my skin.   *I smile*

6. Breathing in, I am aware of the state of my hair.

   Breathing out, I smile to the state of my hair.

   state of
   hair

   I smile

7. Breathing in, I am aware of the state of my heart.

   Breathing out, I smile to the state of my heart.

   state of
   heart

   I smile

8. Breathing in, I am aware of the state of my lungs.

   Breathing out, I smile to the state of my lungs.

   state of lungs

   I smile

9. Breathing in, I am aware of the state of my liver.

   Breathing in, I smile to the state of my liver.

   state of liver

   I smile

10. Breathing in, I am aware of the state of my intestines.

    Breathing out, I smile to the state of my intestines.

    state of
    intestines

    I smile

11. Breathing in, I am aware of the state of my kidneys.

    Breathing out, I smile to the state of my kidneys.

    state of kidneys

    I smile

12. Breathing in, I care for my heart.   *care for heart*

    Breathing out, I smile to my heart.   *smile to heart*

13. Breathing in, I care for my lungs.   *care for lungs*

    Breathing out, I smile to my lungs.   *smile to lungs*

14. Breathing in, I care for my liver.   *care for liver*

    Breathing out, I smile to my liver.   *smile to liver*

15. Breathing in, I care for my intestines.   *care for intestines*

    Breathing out, I smile to my intestines.   *smile to intestines*

16. Breathing in, I care for my kidneys.   *care for kidneys*

    Breathing out, I smile to my kidneys.   *smile to kidneys*

17. Breathing in, I care for my brain.   *care for brain*

    Breathing out, I smile to my brain.   *smile to brain*

This exercise takes us a step further than the previous one. Not only are we in touch with the organs of our body, but we are aware at the same time of the condition of each one. This is a form of compassion meditation whose object is our body. It helps us send our concern and our compassion to them, and teaches us to live mindfully in order to protect our health and the peace and joy of our bodies. It is an invitation to eat, drink, sleep, rest, and work mindfully each day so as not to bring toxins into our bodies. It reminds us not to work the parts of the body (heart, intestines, kidneys, and so on) to exhaustion but to allow them to rest, refresh, and restore their capacity to function well.

EXERCISE 7
Toxins That I Bring into My Body

---

1. Breathing in, I am aware of my physical health.   *my physical health*

    Breathing out, I smile to my physical health.   *I smile*

2. Breathing in, I see toxins in my body. *(toxins from sugar, smoking, alcohol, fats, medication, or any other item of consumption)*   *toxins in my body*

    Breathing out, I know these toxins exhaust my body.   *exhaust my body*

3. Breathing in, I see myself bringing these toxins into my body every day.   *bringing toxins in every day*

    Breathing out, I know these toxins accumulate in my body every day.   *toxins accumulate every day*

4. Breathing in, I see the need to consume mindfully.   *consume mindfully*

    Breathing out, I am determined to follow a healthy diet and abstain from toxic substances.   *abstain from toxic substances*

This exercise goes along with the preceding one. It may help to put a piece of paper and pencil in front of you as you meditate and write down your insights into what you have determined to consume. You can always ask your friends, your sangha, or your close family to support you. If the whole family can go together in the direction of mindful consumption, the practice will be much easier for everyone.

EXERCISE 8

Meditation on the Stages of Decomposition of My Own Corpse

1. Breathing in, I am aware of my body alive and breathing.   *my body alive*

   Breathing out, I smile to my body alive and breathing.   *I smile*

2. Breathing in, I see my corpse lying on a bed.   *my corpse on a bed*

   Breathing out, I smile to my corpse lying on a bed.   *I smile*

3. Breathing in, I see my corpse in a shroud.   *my corpse in a shroud*

   Breathing out, I smile to my corpse in a shroud.   *I smile*

4. Breathing in, I see my corpse being placed in a coffin.   *my corpse in a coffin*

   Breathing out, I smile to my corpse being placed in a coffin.   *I smile*

5. Breathing in, I see my corpse become grey.   *corpse greying*

   Breathing out, I smile to my greying corpse.   *I smile*

6. Breathing in, I see my corpse infested with maggots and flies. *corpse infested*

   Breathing out, I smile to my corpse infested with maggots and flies. *I smile*

7. Breathing in, I see the decomposition of my flesh.   *decomposition of flesh*

   Breathing out, I smile to the decomposition of my flesh.   *I smile*

8. Breathing in, I see my corpse reduced to a white skeleton.   *white skeleton*

   Breathing out, I smile to my corpse reduced to a white skeleton. *I smile*

9. Breathing in, I see my bones no longer held together by ligaments. *dismembered skeleton*

   Breathing out, I smile to my bones no longer held together by ligaments. *I smile*

10. Breathing in, I see my corpse has become a heap of dried bones. *heap of dried bones*

    Breathing out, I smile to the heap of dried bones.   *I smile*

11. Breathing in, I see the bones becoming dust.

    Breathing out, I smile to the bones becoming dust.

    bones become dust

    I smile

12. Breathing in, I see my corpse being cremated.

    Breathing out, I smile to my corpse being cremated.

    corpse cremated

    I smile

13. Breathing in, I see my corpse reduced to ashes.

    Breathing out, I smile to my corpse reduced to ashes.

    reduced to ashes

    I smile

This exercise helps us become accustomed to the fact that sooner or later we all have to die. It is also a way of meditating on the impermanence of the body. It is traditionally known as the "Nine Contemplations on the Unclean" (navāśubha samjñā). If we can become familiar and smile to our fear of death, we shall begin to transform that fear. We shall also begin to live our life more deeply and with more care and awareness so as not to waste it.

When we can envision and accept our own death, we are able to let go of many ambitions, worries, and sufferings. In short, we are able to let go of all the things that keep us so unnecessarily busy. We can begin to live in a way that is meaningful for ourselves and for other species.

The various stages of decomposition of the corpse that belong to the traditional Nine Contemplations can be replaced by simple images more appropriate to our own era. For example, a shroud, coffin, cremation furnace, vase of ashes, ashes becoming earth, or ashes scattered on the waves of a river or ocean.

The exercises on the visualization of a corpse, either one's own or that of another, should only be practiced when the meditator is strong in body and in mind.

EXERCISE 9

Meditation on the Stages of Decomposition of the Corpse of a Loved One

1. Breathing in, I am aware of my beloved alive and healthy.   *beloved alive*

   Breathing out, I smile to my beloved alive and healthy.   *I smile*

2. Breathing in, I see the corpse of my beloved lying on a bed.   *corpse of beloved*

   Breathing out, I smile to the corpse of my beloved lying on a bed.   *I smile*

3. Breathing in, I see the corpse of my beloved become grey.   *beloved, a greying corpse*

   Breathing out, I smile to the greying corpse of my beloved.   *I smile*

4. Breathing in, I see the bloated corpse of my beloved.   *beloved, a bloated corpse*

   Breathing out, I smile to the bloated corpse of my beloved.   *I smile*

5. Breathing in, I see the festering corpse of my beloved.

   beloved, a festering corpse

   Breathing out, I smile to the festering corpse of my beloved.

   I smile

6. Breathing in, I see the corpse of my beloved infested with maggots and flies.

   beloved, a corpse with maggots and flies

   Breathing out, I smile to the corpse of my beloved infested with maggots and flies.

   I smile

7. Breathing in, I see my beloved as a white skeleton.

   beloved, white skeleton

   Breathing out, I smile to my beloved as a white skeleton.

   I smile

8. Breathing in, I see my beloved as bones no longer held together by ligaments.

   beloved, bones without ligaments

   Breathing out, I smile to my beloved as bones no longer held together by ligaments.

   I smile

9. Breathing in, I see my beloved as a heap of dried bones.

   beloved, heap of dried bones

   Breathing out, I smile to my beloved as a heap of dried bones.

   I smile

10. Breathing in, I see my beloved as bones turning to dust.

    beloved, bones turning to dust

    Breathing out, I smile to my beloved as bones turning to dust.

    I smile

This exercise helps us to accept that sooner or later, those we love most will pass away. There is no escaping that fact. As in the preceding exercise, the images presented by the Nine Contemplations can be replaced by simpler ones more appropriate to our time, such as the shroud, coffin, cremation, funeral urn, or ashes spread on the earth or scattered on water.

When we can envision the death of someone we love, we are able to let go of anger and reproachful feelings toward that person. We learn to live in a kinder way with those we love, to look after them, bringing them joy and happiness. Awareness of the impermanence of our loved one will stay alive in us, and we shall be more skillful in our words, thoughts, and actions. We shall avoid hurting our loved ones and sowing seeds of suffering in them.

The meditator should be warned not to visualize the corpse of someone who has already passed away. The practice is to help us face the fear that one day our loved one must die; it is not to relive the experience that we had when we saw the corpse of our loved one.

EXERCISE 10

Meditation on the Stages of Decomposition of the Corpse of the One I Am Angry With

1. Breathing in, I see the one who makes me angry alive and well.

    one who makes me angry, alive, well

    Breathing out, I smile to the one who makes me angry alive and well.

    I smile

2. Breathing in, I see the corpse of the one who makes me angry on its deathbed.

    one who makes me angry, a corpse

    Breathing out, I smile to the corpse of the one who makes me angry on its deathbed.

    I smile

3. Breathing in, see the greying corpse
of the one who makes me angry.

*one who makes
me angry a
greying corpse*

Breathing out, I smile to the greying
corpse of the one who makes me angry.

I smile

4. Breathing in, I see the bloated corpse
of the one who makes me angry.

*one who makes
me angry, a
bloated corpse*

Breathing out, I smile to the bloated
corpse of the one who makes me angry.

I smile

5. Breathing in, I see the festering corpse
of the one who makes me angry.

*one who makes
me angry, a
festering corpse*

Breathing out, I smile to the festering
corpse of the one who makes me angry.

I smile

6. Breathing in, I see the corpse of the
one who makes me angry infested with
maggots and flies.

*one who makes
me angry, corpse
infested with
maggots and
flies*

Breathing out, I smile to the corpse of
the one who makes me angry infested
with maggots and flies.

I smile

7. Breathing in, I see the white skeleton
of the one who makes me angry.

*one who makes
me angry, a
white skeleton*

Breathing out, I smile to the white
skeleton of the one who makes me angry.

I smile

8. Breathing in, I see the one who makes   *one who makes*
    me angry as bones no longer held   *me angry,*
    together by ligaments.   *bones without*
                                                   ligaments

    Breathing out, I smile to the one who   *I smile*
    makes me angry as bones no longer
    held together by ligaments.

9. Breathing in, I see the one who makes   *one who makes*
    me angry as a heap of dried bones.   *me angry, a*
                                                   heap of dried
                                                   bones

    Breathing out, I smile to the one who   *I smile*
    makes me angry as a heap of dried bones.

10. Breathing in, I see the one who makes   *one who makes*
    me angry is now only bones turning   *me angry, bones*
    to dust.   *turning to dust*

    Breathing out, I smile to the one   *I smile*
    who makes me angry as bones turning
    to dust.

This exercise is just like the two that precede it, but the object of the meditation is someone whom we hate or who fills us with anger. We meditate in order to be able to see the frailty and the impermanence of those who hurt us. This meditation will dissolve our anger and foster love and compassion for someone we hate, and for ourselves, too. Very often those with whom we become the most angry are those we love the most. It is precisely because we love someone that we become angry with them.

EXERCISE 11

The No-Birth, No-Death,
and Interbeing Nature of My Eyes

1. Breathing in, I am aware of my eyes.   *my eyes*

   Breathing out, I smile to my eyes.   *I smile*

2. Breathing in, I see my eyes arise from the four elements.   *eyes from four elements*

   Breathing out, I see my eyes dissolve into the four elements.   *dissolve into four elements*

3. Breathing in, I see my eyes contain the sunshine.   *eyes contain sunshine*

   Breathing out, I see my eyes contain the clouds.   *eyes contain cloud*

4. Breathing in, I see my eyes contain the earth.   *eyes contain earth*

   Breathing out, I see my eyes contain the air.   *eyes contain air*

5. Breathing in, I see my eyes contain the whole cosmos.   *eyes contain cosmos*

   Breathing out, I see my eyes present in everything in the cosmos.   *eyes in every-thing in cosmos*

6. Breathing in, I see the interbeing nature of my eyes.   *interbeing of eyes*

   Breathing out, I see the interbeing nature of everything in the cosmos.   *interbeing of all in cosmos*

7. Breathing in, I see the all in the one.   *all in one*

Breathing out, I see the one in the all.   *one in all*

8. Breathing in, I see the one as basic to   *one as basic*
the all.   *to all*

Breathing out, I see all things as basic   *all as basic*
to the one.   *to one*

9. Breathing in, I see the birthless nature   *birthless nature*
of my eyes.   *of eyes*

Breathing out, I see the deathless nature   *deathless nature*
of my eyes.   *of eyes*

The purpose of this exercise and exercise 13 of this chapter is to help us look deeply at the conditioned arising of all things, as well as the interdependence and interpenetration of all that exists.

All that exists is impermanent. If something is born, it must die, and this birth and death is taking place in every instant (in Sanskrit, *ksana,* "the shortest instant of time"). We realize this each time we meditate on impermanence. However, if we look deeper still, we shall see that impermanence means all things arise in dependence on each other. All that exists comes to be, endures, and disappears because of certain causes and conditions: This is because that is. This is not because that is not. This is born because that is born. This ceases to be because that ceases to be. This is the principle of dependent arising, which is taught in the Madhyama and Samyukta Āgamas. As we continue to look deeply, we see that because everything arises in dependence on something else, there is no such thing as a separately existing self-nature. We come to see that all things are in essence empty; empty of a separate self. This contains that and that contains this is the principle of interpenetration. This is that and that is this is the principle of interbeing.

Time contains time, and time contains space. Space contains space, and space contains time. Space is itself time. Space and time cannot exist separately from each other. One ksana (point instant) contains infinite time, and the smallest particle contains limitless space. This is the principle of all is one and one is all. When we understand that principle, the phenomena that we used to call birth, death, being, and nonbeing are seen to be illusions. We are able to see into the birthless and deathless nature of reality, which is sometimes called dharmadhātu (the true nature of the phenomenal world), tathata (suchness), or nirvana (extinction of illusion and sorrow, and ultimate truth). Concepts of birth and death, one and many, coming and going, purity and defilement, and increasing and decreasing cannot be used to describe reality. Only when we realize the birthless and deathless nature of reality will we overcome fear, attachment, and suffering. That realization is liberation.

Exercises 11 and 13 in this chapter need to be practiced diligently, not just during times of sitting meditation but throughout our daily lives.

EXERCISE 12

The Six Elements in Me and in the Universe

---

1. Breathing in, I am aware of my body.   *aware of body*

   Breathing out, I smile to my body.   *I smile*

2. Breathing in, I am aware of the element   *earth element*
   earth in me.   *in me*

   Breathing out, I smile to the element   *I smile*
   earth in me.

3. Breathing in, I am aware of the element   *water element*
   water in me.   *in me*

   Breathing out, I smile to the element   *I smile*
   water in me.

4. Breathing in, I am aware of the element   *fire element*
   fire in me.   *in me*

   Breathing out, I smile to the element   *I smile*
   fire in me.

5. Breathing in, I am aware of the element   *air element*
   air in me.   *in me*

   Breathing out, I smile to the element   *I smile*
   air in me.

6. Breathing in, I am aware of the element   *element space*
   space in me.   *in me*

   Breathing out, I smile to the element   *I smile*
   space in me.

7. Breathing in, I am aware of the element   *element*
   consciousness in me.   *consciousness*

   Breathing out, I smile to the element   *I smile*
   consciousness in me.

8. Breathing in, I recognize the element   *element earth*
   earth everywhere.   *everywhere*

   Breathing out, I smile to the element   *I smile*
   earth everywhere.

9. Breathing in, I see that the element   *earth con-*
   earth contains water, fire, air, space,   *tains the other*
   and consciousness.   *elements*

   Breathing out, I see that earth is water,   *earth is other*
   fire, air, space, and consciousness.   *elements*

10. Breathing in, I recognize the element
    water everywhere.

    element water
    everywhere

    Breathing out, I smile to the element
    water everywhere.

    I smile

11. Breathing in, I see that the element
    water contains earth, fire, air, space,
    and consciousness.

    water con-
    tains the other
    elements

    Breathing out, I see that water is earth,
    fire, air, space, and consciousness.

    water is other
    elements

12. Breathing in, I recognize the element
    fire everywhere.

    element fire
    everywhere

    Breathing out, I smile to the element
    fire everywhere.

    I smile

13. Breathing in, I see that the element
    fire contains earth, water, air, space,
    and consciousness.

    fire contains
    other elements

    Breathing out, I see that fire is earth,
    water, air, space, and consciousness.

    fire is other
    elements

14. Breathing in, I recognize the element
    air everywhere.

    element air
    everywhere

    Breathing out, I smile to the element
    air everywhere.

    I smile

15. Breathing in, I see that the element
    air contains earth, water, fire, space,
    and consciousness.

    air contains
    other elements

    Breathing out, I see that air is earth,
    water, fire, space, and consciousness.

    air is other
    elements

16. Breathing in, I recognize the element space everywhere.

    element space everywhere

    Breathing out, I smile to the element space everywhere.

    I smile

17. Breathing in, I see that the element space contains earth, water, fire, air, and consciousness.

    space contains other elements

    Breathing out, I see that space is earth, water, fire, air, and consciousness.

    space is other elements

18. Breathing in, I recognize the element consciousness everywhere.

    element consciousness everywhere

    Breathing out, I smile to the element consciousness everywhere.

    I smile

19. Breathing in, I see that the element consciousness contains earth, water, air, fire, and space.

    consciousness contains other elements

    Breathing out, I see that consciousness is earth, water, air, fire, and space.

    consciousness is other elements

This exercise leads us to the observation of the six elements that comprise both the human organism and the universe. The six elements are earth, water, fire, air, space, and consciousness. Earth stands for the solid aspect of things, water for the fluid, fire for warmth and heat, air for movement. Space and consciousness are the nature and frame of the four first elements.

When we breathe in, we see earth in our bodies. When we

breathe out, we recognize and smile to that element earth. Earth is the mother who gave us birth, and our mother is right inside us. We are one with our mother; we are one with the earth. Every moment, earth is entering us. The vegetables we eat are also earth. As we meditate, we should see earth by means of concrete images.

When we meditate on water in ourselves, we should see water in our blood, in our saliva, bile, sweat, and urine, and we smile to this water. Our bodies are approximately 70 percent water.

We continue by seeing heat, air, and space in our bodies. If we look deeply, we shall see that these elements all depend on each other. The air—to be precise, the oxygen in the air—is produced by the trees in the forest, and the forest needs the carbon in the air to nourish itself. The vegetable world, including the vegetables we eat, requires the earth and the light and heat of the sun to grow. Neither space nor solid matter could exist without the other. The sutra teaches that form is also mind, and we see consciousness has penetrated every cell of our bodies. Consciousness upholds body, and body upholds consciousness.

When we begin to meditate on earth, water, fire, air, space, and consciousness outside our bodies, we recognize that these six elements are everywhere in the universe. We gradually come to see that we and the universe are one. The universe is our basis, and we are the basis of the universe. The composition and the decomposition of a body do not add or take away anything from the universe. The sun is just as necessary for our bodies as are our hearts. The forest is just as necessary for our bodies as are our lungs. Our bodies need the river as much as they need our blood. If we continue to meditate like this, we shall see that we can let go of the boundaries between "I" and "not I," and thus we can overcome the distinction between birth and death, being and nonbeing, and finally we can conquer fear. According to the principle of interdependent origination, the one comes about because of the all, and the all is present in the one. Thus the earth element contains the five other elements: water, heat, air, space, and consciousness. The earth element can be recognized as including the whole universe within itself. The Pali word kasina (in Sanskrit, *krtsna*) is sometimes translated as "sign," meaning the sign that we have realized the object of our meditation. However, the original meaning of the word is "wholeness." When our meditation is deep enough, we see that each element contains all the others. Such a practice is called krtsnāyatanabhāvanā, which means "meditations for entering the whole." In krtsnāyatanabhāvanā, we can also meditate on colors: blue, red, white, and yellow. These four colors and the six elements make up ten meditations for entering the whole. Colors are also present in the universe and in us, and every color contains all the other colors and also contains the six elements that are in us and in the whole universe.

EXERCISE 13

Contemplating the No-Birth, No-Death Nature of My Body

1. Breathing in, I am aware of my in-breath. *in-breath*

    Breathing out, I see my in-breath no longer there. *in-breath not there*

2. Breathing in, I am aware of the birth of my in-breath. *birth of in-breath*

    Breathing out, I am aware of the death of my in-breath. *death of in-breath*

3. Breathing in, I see my in-breath born from conditions. *in-breath born from conditions*

    Breathing out, I see my in-breath die from conditions. *in-breath dies because of conditions*

4. Breathing in, I see my in-breath comes
    from nowhere.

    *in-breath comes
    from nowhere*

    Breathing out, I see my in-breath
    goes nowhere.

    *in-breath goes
    nowhere*

5. Breathing in, I see my in-breath is
    not born, does not die.

    *in-breath not
    born does not die*

    Breathing out, I see my in-breath
    free from birth and death.

    *free from birth
    and death*

6. Breathing in, I am aware of my eyes.

    aware of eyes

    Breathing out, I see my eyes born
    from conditions.

    *eyes born from
    conditions*

7. Breathing in, I see my eyes come from
    nowhere.

    *eyes come from
    nowhere*

    Breathing out, I see my eyes go nowhere.

    eyes go nowhere

8. Breathing in, I see my eyes have no
    birth and death.

    *eyes have no
    birth, no death*

    Breathing out, I see my eyes free from
    birth and death.

    *free from birth,
    death*

9. Breathing in, I am aware of my body.

    aware of body

    Breathing out, I see my body born
    from conditions.

    *born from
    conditions*

10. Breathing in, I see my body comes
    from nowhere.

    *body comes
    from nowhere*

    Breathing out, I see my body goes
    nowhere.

    *body goes
    nowhere*

11. Breathing in, I see my body has no
    birth and death.

    Breathing out, I see my body free
    from birth and death.

    body has no
    birth, no death

    free from birth
    and death

12. Breathing in, I am aware of my
    consciousness.

    Breathing out, I see my consciousness
    born from conditions.

    consciousness

    born from
    conditions

13. Breathing in, I see my consciousness
    comes from nowhere.

    Breathing out, I see my consciousness
    goes nowhere.

    consciousness
    comes from
    nowhere

    goes nowhere

14. Breathing in, I see my consciousness
    has no birth and death.

    Breathing out, I see my consciousness
    free from birth and death.

    consciousness
    has no birth, no
    death

    free from birth
    and death

This exercise helps us to realize that nothing comes and nothing goes, nothing is born and nothing dies. This is one of the most wonderful meditation practices in Buddhism.

To start with, we observe the presence of each breath in order to be aware of the birth and the death of that breath. As we begin to breathe in, we see the in-breath being born, and as we begin to breathe out, we see the in-breath has died. Birth and death are two marks or signs (in Sanskrit, *lakshana*) that can define the life span of a breath. As we continue the meditation, we see that the occurrence of our in-breath is dependent on various causes and conditions: the lungs, the respiratory muscles, the body, the atmosphere, the nose, the bronchial tubes, being alive, and so on.

As we breathe out, we see that the death of the in-breath is also due to causes and conditions, and we become physically aware of those conditions. For example, the lungs are now full of air and are not able or do not want to breathe in anymore. As we meditate, we see that when the causes and conditions are right, the breath is born, and when the right causes and conditions are not present, it dies. We see that our breath at its birth does not come from anywhere and at its death does not go anywhere. There is no place in space where it comes from when it is born, and there is no place in space it goes to when it dies. Then we see the not-coming, not-going nature of the breath.

Looking more deeply, we see that a breath is not born and does not die, but only manifests itself or lies hidden.

Being born usually means that something comes into existence that did not exist before. Dying usually means something that has existed ceases to exist. But our breath is not like that. We cannot say that it did not exist before, only that once the conditions are sufficient, it can manifest itself. If one of those conditions is absent, the breath goes into hiding. It is with regard to our perception that we talk about manifesting and failing to manifest.

Manifest does not mean that something exists and not manifest does not mean that something fails to exist. Markers like birth and death, being and nonbeing, are assigned to the breath by our perception. The true nature of all things is that of no-birth, no-death, no-existence, no-nonexistence. The realization of this arises with our willingness to persevere in looking deeply into causes and conditions.

When we meditate on our eyes, we see that our eyes, too, manifest dependent on conditions and go into hiding dependent on conditions. Our eyes do not come from anywhere and do not go away to any place. Eyes manifesting does not mean that eyes exist, and eyes going into hiding does not mean that eyes fail to exist. We cannot say that our eyes are born because they manifest, and we cannot say that they die because they fail to manifest. The same is true of our bodies and our consciousness. The true nature of the five aggregates (body, feelings, perceptions, mental formations, and consciousness) is no-birth, no-death, no-existence, and no-nonexistence. Birth and death are both illusory. To be, or not to be: that is not the question.

EXERCISE 14

The No-Birth, No-Death Nature of the Ocean Water and Myself

---

1. Breathing in, I am aware of a wave on the ocean. *ocean wave*

    Breathing out, I smile to the wave on the ocean. *I smile*

2. Breathing in, I am aware of the water in the wave. *water in wave*

    Breathing out, I smile to the water in the wave. *I smile*

3. Breathing in, I see the birth of a wave. *birth of wave*

    Breathing out, I smile to the birth of the wave. *I smile*

4. Breathing in, I see the death of a wave. *death of wave*

    Breathing out, I smile to the death of the wave. *I smile*

5. Breathing in, I see the birthless nature   *birthless nature*
    of the water in the wave.   *of water*

    Breathing out, I smile to the birthless   *I smile*
    nature of the water in the wave.

6. Breathing in, I see the deathless nature   *deathless nature*
    of the water in the wave.   *of water*

    Breathing out, I smile to the deathless   *I smile*
    nature of the water in the wave.

7. Breathing in, I see the birth of my body.   *birth of body*

    Breathing out, I smile to the birth of   *I smile*
    my body.

8. Breathing in, I see the death of my body.   *death of body*

    Breathing out, I smile to the death of   *I smile*
    my body.

9. Breathing in, I see the birthless nature   *birthless nature*
    of my body.   *of body*

    Breathing out, I smile to the birthless   *I smile*
    nature of my body.

10. Breathing in, I see the deathless nature   *deathless nature*
    of my body.   *of body*

    Breathing out, I smile to the deathless   *I smile*
    nature of my body.

11. Breathing in, I see the birthless nature   *birthless nature*
of my consciousness.   *of consciousness*

Breathing out, I smile to the birthless   *I smile*
nature of my consciousness.

12. Breathing in, I see the deathless nature   *deathless nature*
of my consciousness.   *of consciousness*

Breathing out, I smile to the deathless   *I smile*
nature of my consciousness.

This exercise goes along with the two preceding exercises, and its aim is to help us look deeply into the true nature of all things.

The phenomenal world seems to be marked by oppositions: birth/death, coming/going, being/nonbeing, one/many, defilement/purity, and so on. When we are able to look deeply into the nature of phenomena, we see beyond such notions as these. The three seals of Buddhist teaching are impermanence, no-self, and nirvana. Impermanence and no-self belong to the phenomenological world. Because the reality of phenomena is impermanence and no-self, we see birth, death, coming, going, enduring, ceasing, same, different, defiled, or pure. But Buddhism does more than reveal the phenomenal aspect of reality; it puts us in touch with the true nature (in Sanskrit, *svabhāva*) of phenomena. That true nature is nirvana. Nirvana cannot be described by means of concepts like birth, death, coming, going, being, non-being. Nirvana means bringing to silence all notions and words. It also means the absence of afflictions like desire, hatred, and ignorance. Once we realize the nature of reality, we can overcome all fear, anxiety, and craving, because the marks of birth, death, coming, going, being, and non-being are seen to be illusions when we have deep understanding.

In the Udāna (Inspired Utterances), Buddha speaks of nirvana in the following way: "Monks, there is a place which is not the place of earth, water, air, or fire, limitless space or limitless consciousness, limitless non-materiality, perceptions or no perceptions, this world or that world. I do not say that there is coming and going or not coming and not going, or being born and dying in this place. In this place there is neither coming into existence or passing away and it does not need to rely on something else. It is the ending of all suffering. It is nirvana." And again in the Udāna: "Monks, there is something which is not born, which is not conditioned, which does not become, is not made, is not a composite. Supposing that this non-born, nonconditioned, not-become, not made, not compounded were not there? How could there be a place for the born, the conditioned, the become, the made, the compounded to return to?"

Suppose that while listening to the Buddha speaking like this, we are caught in the words, "There is a place." Then we shall not be able to understand him, because the reality of nirvana goes beyond all ideas of *is* or *is not, one* or *many, place* and *no place, this* and *that.* Let us be very careful not to be caught in words and ideas, because the Buddha has also taught that it is impossible to say anything about the true nature of nirvana.

This exercise uses the image of a wave and the water as a metaphor for nirvana. The wave is birth and death; the water is nirvana. The wave is born and dies, rises and falls, is high and is low, comes to be and passes away, is many and is one. This is not true of the water in the wave. We should remember that this is only a metaphor. In our common perception, water still belongs to the phenomenal world, like clouds, vapor, ice, and snow.

Because we are able to look deeply at the phenomenal world, we are able to discover its birthless and deathless nature and to enter the world of suchness. In Buddhist studies, we talk about the process of going from the mark (*laksana*) to the nature (*svabhāva*), from the sign to the essence.

A bodhisattva is able to see the nature of all that is and therefore has no more fear or craving. Thus they can ride on the waves of birth and death and smile to the waves as they are born and die.

CHAPTER 2

Feelings and Mental Formations

his chapter treats the second and third establishments of mindfulness. Based on exercises 5–8, concerning the feelings, and 9–12, concerning the mind, from the Anapanasati Sutta[1] exercises, we propose eleven exercises in this chapter.

EXERCISE 1
Restoring Beauty in Myself

1. Breathing in, I know I am breathing in.   *in*

   Breathing out, I know I am breathing   *out*
   out.

2. Breathing in, I see myself as a flower.   *flower*

   Breathing out, I feel fresh.   *fresh*

3. Breathing in, I see myself as a mountain.   *mountain*

   Breathing out, I feel solid.   *solid*

1. See "The Sixteen Exercises of the Sutta on the Full Awareness of Breathing," p. 121.

4. Breathing in, I see myself as still water.   *still water*

   Breathing out, I reflect all that is.   *reflecting*

5. Breathing in, I see myself as space.   *space*

   Breathing out, I feel free.   *free*

When we meditate, we use our store consciousness (the deepest levels of our consciousness) more than our mind consciousness (thinking and rationalization). That is why images are more useful to the meditator than abstract concepts. These exercises are to help us be aware of and nourished by the contact of the five senses with the sense objects. They help us to appreciate more the wonders of life that our senses make possible. They also help us be aware of any feelings—pleasant, unpleasant, or neutral—that arise when our senses touch sense objects.

This exercise can be practiced in the first part of any period of sitting meditation, or for the whole of the meditation period, to nourish and calm body and mind, to enable the meditator to let go and attain freedom.

The first stage should be practiced for as long as it takes the body and mind to become one. The second stage encourages a sense of freshness. A human being should be as fresh as a flower, for indeed we are one species of flower in the garden of all phenomena. We need only to look at the beauty of children to see that human beings are flowers. Two bright eyes are flowers. The clear complexion of the face with its gentle forehead is a flower. Their two hands are flowers. . . . It is only because we worry that our foreheads become wrinkled. It is only because we cry so much and pass so many sleepless nights that our eyes lose their sparkle. We breathe in to restore the flower in us. This in-breath brings our flower back to life. The out-breath helps us be aware that we have the capacity to be, and are now, fresh as a flower. This awareness waters our flower. It is the practice of loving-kindness meditation toward ourselves.

The third stage, "mountain, solid," helps us to stand firmly when we are upset by vehement feelings. Whenever we feel despair, anxiety, fear, or anger, we are carried right into the heart of a whirlwind. We are like a tree standing in a gale. If we look up, we shall see our branches bending as if they are about to break and be carried away by the storm. But if we look down at the trunk and the roots, we shall know that the roots of the tree are held firmly in the earth, and we shall feel more stable and relaxed.

Body and mind are like that. When there is a hurricane of emotions in us, if we know how to withdraw from the storm—that is, if we know how to withdraw from the turmoil in our brain—we shall not be swept away. We must transfer our attention to a place in the abdomen called the *tantien* acupoint (about four fingers' width below the navel) and breathe deeply and slowly according to the formula "mountain, solid." In doing this, we shall see that we are not just our emotions. Emotions come and go, but we shall remain. When we are oppressed by emotions, we feel very insecure and fragile; we may feel that we are in danger of losing life itself. Some people do not know how to deal with their strong emotions. When they are suffering greatly from despair, fear, or anger, they think the only way to put an end to their suffering is to put an end to their life. But those who know how to sit in meditation and practice breathing with the exercise "mountain, solid" can weather such times of difficulty and suffering.

This exercise can also be practiced as we lie on our back. We can direct our attention to the rising and falling of the lower abdomen and keep it there. This will enable us to leave the storm and not fall back into it. We practice this abdominal breathing until our heart and mind have calmed down and the storm has passed. However, we should not wait until we find ourselves in difficulty to practice. If we have not cultivated the habit of practicing, we shall not know what to do, and our emotions may once again overwhelm and oppress us. To make a good habit, we can practice every day; in that way, whenever painful feelings arise, we shall know quite naturally how to transform them. In addition, we can explain this practice to young people to help them not be victims of their strong emotions.

"Still water, reflecting" is the fourth stage helping us calm body and mind. In the Anapanasati Sutta, the Buddha taught: "Breathing in, I make my mind calm. . . ." This exercise essentially does the same; the image of still water in a lake, for example, simply makes the practice easier. When our mind is agitated, our perceptions are usually clouded; what we see, hear, and think does not reflect the reality of things, just as when the surface of a lake is unsettled by waves, it cannot clearly reflect the clouds above. I wrote this gatha based on the words of our ancestral teachers:

> *Buddha is like the cool moon,*
> *Crossing the immense clear sky.*
> *When the lake of the mind is calm,*
> *The moon reflects beautifully in it.*

Our sorrows, pains, and anger arise from our wrong perceptions. In order to avoid these wrong perceptions, we need to practice making the mind as still as the surface of a lake on an autumn morning. Mindful breathing is what does that.

If we have too many preoccupations and worries, we will not have clarity, peace, and joy. "Space, free," the fifth stage, is to create space in our hearts and around us. We train ourselves to release the projects and anxiety that burden us. We can do the same for our sorrows and anger. We can practice letting go of the things we carry needlessly. This sort of baggage only makes life heavy, even if sometimes we think we cannot be happy without it—without, for example, a title, high position, fame, a successful business, and people to run around after us. But if we look again, we shall see that this baggage is often nothing but an obstacle to our happiness. If we can just put it down, we shall have happiness.

Buddha is like the cool moon,
Crossing the immense clear sky. . . .

The immense clear sky is the sky of limitless space. That is why the happiness of the Buddha is so great. One day, the Buddha was sitting in the forest at Vaisali and he saw a farmer going past. The farmer asked the Buddha if he had seen his herd of cows, which had broken loose. He also complained that earlier that year, he had lost two acres of sesame fields when they were attacked by caterpillars, and lamented that he must be the most wretched person on earth. Perhaps, he added, he should put an end to his own life. The Buddha said they had not seen any cows and with great compassion advised him to look in another direction. After the farmer had gone, the Buddha turned to the bhiksus who were sitting with him and smiled. He said: "Bhiksus, are you aware of your happiness and freedom? You do not have any cows to lose." Practicing this last exercise helps us to let go of our cows, the cows of our mind and the cows we have gathered around us. It also can be sung.[2]

EXERCISE 2
I Have Arrived. I Am Home.

1. Breathing in, I know I am breathing in.   *in*

   Breathing out, I know I am breathing   *out*
   out.

2. Breathing in, I am aware of my whole   *aware of body*
   body.

   Breathing out, I release the tensions   *releasing all*
   in my body.   *tensions*

2. For all songs, please refer to http://plumvillage.org/library/songs/.

3. Breathing in, I am at home.   *at home*

Breathing out, I feel at ease.   *at ease*

4. Breathing in, I have arrived.   *arrived*

Breathing out, no more need to run.   *no need to run*

5. Breathing in, I dwell in the here.   *here*

Breathing out, I dwell in the now.   *now*

6. Breathing in, I feel solid.   *solid*

Breathing out, I am truly free.   *free*

7. Breathing in, I have confidence in myself.   *confidence in myself*

Breathing out, I take refuge in myself.   *refuge in myself*

Song: I have arrived. I am home.[3]

EXERCISE 3

Nourishing and Healing Myself with the Wonders of Life

---

1. Breathing in, I am in touch with the   *pure air*
    pure air.

Breathing out, I smile with the pure air.   *I smile*

---

3. For all songs, please refer to http://plumvillage.org/library/songs/.

2. Breathing in, I am in touch with pure mountain air.

    pure mountain air

    Breathing out, I smile with pure mountain air.

    I smile

3. Breathing in, I am in touch with pure countryside air.

    pure countryside air

    Breathing out, I smile with the pure countryside air.

    I smile

4. Breathing in, I am in touch with cool water.

    cool water

    Breathing out, I smile with the cool water.

    I smile

5. Breathing in, I am in touch with a clear stream.

    clear stream

    Breathing out, I smile with the clear stream.

    I smile

6. Breathing in, I am in touch with snow on a mountain peak.

    snow on mountain

    Breathing out, I smile with the snow on a mountain peak.

    I smile

7. Breathing in, I am in touch with the vast ocean.

    vast ocean

    Breathing out, I smile with the vast ocean.

    I smile

8. Breathing in, I am in touch with Arctic   *Arctic ice fields*
   ice fields.

   Breathing out, I smile with Arctic ice   *I smile*
   fields.

9. Breathing in, I am in touch with clouds   *clouds in blue*
   in the blue sky.   *sky*

   Breathing out, I smile with clouds in   *I smile*
   the blue sky.

10. Breathing in, I am in touch with warm   *warm sunshine*
    sunshine.

    Breathing out, I smile with the warm   *I smile*
    sunshine.

11. Breathing in, I am in touch with green   *green trees*
    trees.

    Breathing out, I smile with the green   *I smile*
    trees.

12. Breathing in, I am in touch with children.   *children*

    Breathing out, I smile with the children.   *I smile*

13. Breathing in, I am in touch with the   *people around*
    people around me.   *me*

    Breathing out, I smile with the people   *I smile*
    around me.

14. Breathing in, I am in touch with the   *birdsong*
    birdsong.

    Breathing out, I smile with the birdsong.   *I smile*

15. Breathing in, I am in touch with the   *blue sky*
    blue sky.

    Breathing out, I smile with the blue sky.   *I smile*

16. Breathing in, I am in touch with flowers.   *flowers*

    Breathing out, I smile with the flowers.   *I smile*

17. Breathing in, I am in touch with the   *spring*
    spring.

    Breathing out, I smile with the spring.   *I smile*

18. Breathing in, I am in touch with the   *summer*
    summer.

    Breathing out, I smile with the summer.   *I smile*

19. Breathing in, I am in touch with the fall.   *fall*

    Breathing out, I smile with the fall.   *I smile*

EXERCISE 4

Nourishing and Healing with Mindfulness of Sense Contact

1. Breathing in, I am aware of my eyes.   *my eyes*

   Breathing out, I am aware of light.   *light*

2. Breathing in, I am aware of my ears.   *my ears*

   Breathing out, I am aware of sound.   *sound*

3. Breathing in, I am aware of my ears.   *my ears*

    Breathing out, I am aware of a cry of pain.   *a cry of pain*

4. Breathing in, I am aware of my ears.   *my ears*

    Breathing out, I am aware of singing.   *singing*

5. Breathing in, I am aware of my ears.   *my ears*

    Breathing out, I am aware of the sound   *sound of rain*
    of rain.

6. Breathing in, I am aware of my ears.   *my ears*

    Breathing out, I am aware of laughter.   *laughter*

7. Breathing in, I am aware of my ears.   *my ears*

    Breathing out, I am aware of silence.   *silence*

8. Breathing in, I am aware of my skin.   *my skin*

    Breathing out, I am aware of the sense   *sense of touch*
    of touch.

9. Breathing in, I am aware of my skin.   *my skin*

    Breathing out, I am aware of the warm   *warm sun*
    sun on my skin.

10. Breathing in, I am aware of my skin.   *my skin*

    Breathing out, I am aware of cool water   *cool water*
    on my skin.

11. Breathing in, I am aware of my skin.   *my skin*

    Breathing out, I am aware of ice on   *ice*
    my skin.

12. Breathing in, I am aware of my skin.   *my skin*

    Breathing out, I am aware of touching   *bark of a tree*
    the bark of a tree.

13. Breathing in, I am aware of my skin.   *my skin*

    Breathing out, I am aware of touching   *an earthworm*
    an earthworm.

14. Breathing in, I am aware of my teeth.   *my teeth*

    Breathing out, I am aware of an apple.   *an apple*

15. Breathing in, I am aware of my teeth.   *my teeth*

    Breathing out, I am aware of a toothache.   *toothache*

16. Breathing in, I am aware of my teeth.   *my teeth*

    Breathing out, I am aware of lemon juice.   *lemon juice*

17. Breathing in, I am aware of my teeth.   *my teeth*

    Breathing out, I am aware of the   *dentist's drill*
    dentist's drill.

18. Breathing in, I am aware of my tongue.   *tongue*

    Breathing out, I am aware of the taste   *orange juice*
    of orange juice.

19. Breathing in, I am aware of my tongue.   *tongue*

    Breathing out, I am aware of the taste   *lemon*
    of lemon.

20. Breathing in, I am aware of my tongue.   *tongue*

    Breathing out, I am aware of the taste   *salt water*
    of salt water.

21. Breathing in, I am aware of my tongue.   *tongue*

    Breathing out, I am aware of the taste   *hot pepper*
    of hot pepper.

22. Breathing in, I am aware of my lungs.   *lungs*

    Breathing out, I am aware of smell.   *smell*

23. Breathing in, I am aware of my lungs.   *lungs*

    Breathing out, I am aware of the scent   *fresh grass*
    of fresh grass.

24. Breathing in, I am aware of my lungs.   *lungs*

    Breathing out, I am aware of the scent   *roses*
    of roses.

25. Breathing in, I am aware of my lungs.   *lungs*

    Breathing out, I am aware of the smell   *dung*
    of dung.

26. Breathing in, I am aware of my lungs.   *lungs*

    Breathing out, I am aware of tobacco   *tobacco smoke*
    smoke.

27. Breathing in, I am aware of my lungs.   *lungs*

    Breathing out, I am aware of the smell   *smell of the sea*
    of the sea.

28. Breathing in, I am aware of my liver.   *liver*

    Breathing out, I am aware of the taste   *taste of wine*
    of wine.

29. Breathing in, I am aware of my liver.   *liver*

    Breathing out, I am aware of greasy food.   *greasy food*

30. Breathing in, I am aware of my liver.   *liver*

    Breathing out, I am aware of yellow   *yellow skin*
    skin caused by a sick liver.

31. Breathing in, I am aware of my feet.   *feet*

    Breathing out, I am aware of shoes.   *shoes*

32. Breathing in, I am aware of my feet.   *feet*

    Breathing out, I am aware of young   *young grass*
    grass.

33. Breathing in, I am aware of my feet.   *feet*

    Breathing out, I am aware of sand on   *sand*
    the beach.

34. Breathing in, I am aware of my feet.   *feet*

    Breathing out, I am aware of a thorn.   *thorn*

35. Breathing in, I am aware of my feet.   *feet*

    Breathing out, I am aware of an anthill.   *anthill*

These two exercises help us to be in contact with wholesome and fresh things, which have the capacity to heal. Our minds are often thrown into a state of confusion by our anxiety and pain, and we have lost the ability to connect with the wonderful things in life. It is as if there is a wall between us and the richness of the world outside, and we have become numb toward the healing elements in the world because we cannot touch them.

In exercise 3, there are examples of sense contacts that give rise to painful feelings. This practice helps us to be mindful when we encounter painful feelings in our daily life and to be less afraid of them.

When we visualize the Arctic ice fields, we may recognize that this is a wonder of nature that is disappearing as global warming increases. This will help us be in touch with impermanence and to strengthen our deep aspiration to do all we can to reverse global warming.

As you practice these two exercises, although you may not be in direct contact with the things you are asked to concentrate upon, you can find them by means of the images stored in your consciousness. These images are in the store consciousness in the form of seeds. You can call them up when you want them to present themselves. With conscious breathing and the power of concentration, contact with these images will help you to discover that your ability to feel is still intact.

After practicing these two exercises, you can go outside in nature and continue to practice being in touch, not just with your mind as in meditation, but with all your senses—eyes, ears, nose, tongue, body. You will see that the outside world is brighter and more beautiful than before, because you have put an end to forgetfulness and have lit the lamp of mindfulness. You have begun again to be nourished by what is wonderful in life.

EXERCISE 5

Recognizing and Embracing Feelings

1. Breathing in, I am aware of my body.   *my body*

   Breathing out, I smile to my body.   *I smile*

2. Breathing in, I experience pain in my   *pain in body*
   body.

   Breathing out, I smile to the pain.   *I smile*

3. Breathing in, I recognize that this is   *pain only*
   only a physical pain.   *physical*

   Breathing out, I know it is impermanent.   *impermanent*

4. Breathing in, I experience pain in my   *pain in mind*
   mind.

   Breathing out, I smile to the pain in   *I smile*
   my mind.

5. Breathing in, I experience my fear.   *fear*

   Breathing out, I smile to the fear.   *I smile*

6. Breathing in, I experience my anxiety.   *anxiety*

   Breathing out, I smile to the anxiety.   *I smile*

7. Breathing in, I experience my sadness.   *sadness*

   Breathing out, I smile to the sadness.   *I smile*

8. Breathing in, I experience my anger.   *anger*

   Breathing out, I smile to the anger.   *I smile*

9. Breathing in, I experience my jealousy.   *jealousy*

   Breathing out, I smile to the jealousy.   *I smile*

10. Breathing in, I experience my craving.   *craving*

   Breathing out, I smile to the craving.   *I smile*

11. Breathing in, I experience excited joy.   *excited joy*

   Breathing out, I smile to the exuberant   *I smile*
   joy.

12. Breathing in, I experience peaceful joy.   *peaceful joy*

   Breathing out, I smile to the peaceful joy.   *I smile*

13. Breathing in, I experience the joy of   *joy of letting go*
   letting go.

   Breathing out, I smile to the joy of   *I smile*
   letting go.

14. Breathing in, I experience the joy of   *joy of freedom*
   freedom.

   Breathing out, I smile to the joy of   *I smile*
   freedom.

15. Breathing in, I experience a neutral   *neutral feeling*
   feeling.

   Breathing out, I smile to the neutral   *I smile*
   feeling.

This exercise is to help us be in touch with all the feelings that arise in our minds. The feelings are either pleasant, unpleasant, or neutral. We must learn to recognize, acknowledge, and smile to each one and to look into its impermanence. A feeling or an emotion arises, persists, and then disappears. Mindfulness enables us to be calm throughout the appearance and disappearance of feelings. Buddha taught us not to be attached to feelings, but also not to push them away. To recognize feelings with an even mind is the best way; while we are acknowledging them in mindfulness, we gradually come to a deep realization of their nature. It is that insight that enables us to be free and at peace with each feeling.

Feelings of fear, anxiety, sadness, anger, jealousy, and craving are often unpleasant or painful. The steady practice of mindfulness will help us to acknowledge the painful feeling whenever it appears. The practice of mere recognition helps us to stay calm, so that we do not drown in powerful waves of feelings or emotions. Sitting in a stable, upright, and relaxed position, we should bring our attention to the part of the abdomen just below the navel. Along with the rising and falling of the abdomen, we should become aware of our in-breath and out-breath for the duration of ten or fifteen minutes. During that time, we shall feel peace of mind being restored, and we shall not be blown away by the gales of emotion. As we continue to acknowledge and look deeply, we shall see the essence of each feeling and emotion as it arises.

We should acknowledge and look deeply at pleasant feelings as well as at painful ones, for states of mind born from freedom, release, and letting go are healthy and nourishing. Acknowledged in mindfulness, these states of mind are able to increase and last longer. Mindful breathing is the wholesome food for these feelings, which are so necessary in our lives.

States of mind are always accompanied by an object of perception. Freedom is freedom from something, and letting go is letting go of something. The meditator should identify the object that he is letting go in order to experience the mental formation and accompanying feeling fully.

A neutral feeling is neither pleasant nor painful. But when such feelings are recognized in mindfulness, they usually become pleasant feelings. This is one of the benefits of insight meditation. When you have a toothache, the feeling is very unpleasant, and when you do not have a toothache, you usually have a neutral feeling. However, if you can be mindful of the non-toothache, the non-toothache will become a feeling of peace and joy. Mindfulness gives rise to and nourishes happiness.

EXERCISE 6

Contemplating the Seeds I Water Every Day

1. Breathing in, I am aware of my mental health.   *my mental health*

   Breathing out, I smile to my state of mental health.   *I smile*

2. Breathing in, I see toxins such as anger, jealousy, violence, fear . . . in my consciousness.   *toxins in my consciousness*

   Breathing out, I know these poisons are harming me and those around me.   *harming me and others*

3. Breathing in, I see how my way of life waters these toxic seeds daily.   *water toxic seeds daily*

   Breathing out, I know that continuing to live like this increases my suffering every day.   *increases suffering daily*

4. Breathing in, I am determined not to   *not watering*
   water these seeds anymore.   *these seeds*

   Breathing out, I am determined to   *stop consuming*
   stop consuming toxic internet sites,   *toxic products*
   television programs, magazines, and
   conversations . . .

This exercise, like exercise 7 of chapter 1, can also be practiced with the help of pencil and paper. The principle is the same. The first stage is to acknowledge the poisons that are already present within us. The second is to recognize the poisons that we bring into our minds daily. In the third stage, we are able to determine what we should or should not do to transform our state of being.

In the first stage, we acknowledge the toxins already present in us such as anger, violence, and fear. We know they are lying in the depths of our consciousness, ready to surface at any time we water them.

In the second stage, we acknowledge the toxins that we are bringing into our consciousness every day. What we listen to or see in films, books, magazines, and conversations can be full of violence, hatred, fear, and craving. Society and collective consciousness are full of violence and hatred. If in our daily lives we do not know how to protect ourselves, the negative seeds will continue to be watered. We need to be aware of what we hear, see, and read every day. We need to be aware of the cultural products we consume and the conversations we have and people we spend time with. We must sincerely ask ourselves what it is that continues to water the toxic seeds within us.

The third stage marks our determination to live in mindfulness to avoid poisoning ourselves anymore. We are determined to end contact with and consumption of all that does us harm. We choose which films to watch and which materials to read, and we are careful in the associations we make and the conversations we have. There are films, books, magazines, and conversations that can water the seeds of happiness, tolerance, compassion, forgiveness . . . It is easier to water the positive seeds and avoid watering the negative ones if those around us, our families or our communities, practice together with us.

The details of the insights we discover in our meditation can be noted clearly on a sheet of paper. This is a way of establishing a healthy diet for living. By following this diet, we shall be able to restore our mental health and recover the joy of being alive. It is most helpful if we can share this exercise with our families or the people with whom we live.

EXERCISE 7

Contemplating the Roots of Our Feelings and Emotions

1. Breathing in, I am aware of my body.   *my body*

    Breathing out, I smile to my body.   *I smile*

2. Breathing in, I am aware of pain in my body.   *pain in body*

    Breathing out, I smile to pain in my body.   *I smile*

3. Breathing in, I see the roots of the pain in my body.   *roots of*

    Breathing out, I smile to the roots of the pain in my body.   *I smile*

4. Breathing in, I am aware of my state of mind.   *my state of mind*

    Breathing out, I smile to my state of mind.   *I smile*

5. Breathing in, I am aware of pain in   *pain in my mind*
    my mind.

    Breathing out, I smile to the pain in   *I smile*
    my mind.

6. Breathing in, I see the roots of the   *roots of pain*
    pain in my mind.

    Breathing out, I smile to the roots   *I smile*
    of pain in my mind.

7. Breathing in, I see the roots of my fear.   *roots of fear*

    Breathing out, I smile to the roots   *I smile*
    of my fear.

8. Breathing in, I see the roots of my   *roots of feeling*
    feeling of insecurity.   *insecure*

    Breathing out, I smile to the roots   *I smile*
    of my feeling of insecurity.

9. Breathing in, I see the roots of my   *roots of sadness*
    sadness.

    Breathing out, I smile to the roots of   *I smile*
    my sadness.

10. Breathing in, I see the roots of my anger.   *roots of anger*

    Breathing out, I smile to the roots of   *I smile*
    my anger.

11. Breathing in, I see the roots of my   *roots of jealousy*
    jealousy.

    Breathing out, I smile to the roots   *I smile*
    of my jealousy.

12. Breathing in, I see the roots of my   *roots of*
    attachment.   *attachment*

    Breathing out, I smile to the roots   *I smile*
    of my attachment.

13. Breathing in, I see the roots of my   *roots of craving*
    craving.

    Breathing out, I smile to the roots   *I smile*
    of my craving.

14. Breathing in, I see the roots of my joy.   *roots of joy*

    Breathing out, I smile to the roots of   *I smile*
    my joy.

15. Breathing in, I see the roots of the joy   *roots of joy of*
    of freedom.   *freedom*

    Breathing out, I smile to the roots of   *I smile*
    the joy of freedom.

16. Breathing in, I see the roots of the joy   *roots of joy of*
    of letting go.   *letting go*

    Breathing out, I smile to the roots of   *I smile*
    the joy of letting go.

17. Breathing in, I see the roots of the joy   *roots of joy of*
    of equanimity.   *equanimity*

    Breathing out, I smile to the roots of   *I smile*
    the joy of equanimity.

18. Breathing in, I see the roots of my   *roots of neutral*
    neutral feelings.   *feeling*

    Breathing out, I smile to the roots   *I smile*
    of my neutral feelings.

To oppose, brush aside, or deny pain in our body or mind only makes that feeling more intense. In the preceding exercises, we have practiced acknowledging and accepting painful feelings. Our painful feelings are not other than ourselves, or to put it more precisely, they are a part of us. To deny them is to deny our very selves. The moment we accept these feelings, we begin to feel more peaceful, and the pain begins to lose some of its intensity. The same happens when we calm our body and relax our muscles: the pain decreases. To smile to our pain is the wisest, the most intelligent, the most beautiful thing we can do. There is no better way.

Every time we acknowledge a feeling of pain and make its acquaintance, we come in closer contact with ourselves. Bit by bit, we look deeply into the nature and the roots of that pain. Fear, insecurity, anger, sadness, jealousy, and attachment form blocks of feelings and thoughts within us (in Sanskrit, *samyojana*, or "internal formation"), and we need time and opportunity to acknowledge them and to look into them. Mindfulness of feeling accompanied by mindful breathing is able to relieve painful feelings. Mindfulness recognizes the presence of the feelings, acknowledges them, soothes them, and enables the work of observation to continue until the nature of the internal formation is seen. This is the only way to transform it. All the seeds of suffering are present within us, and if we live in forgetfulness, or in an unwholesome environment, these seeds will be watered every day. They will grow strong and become large blocks of suffering. The practice can transform these internal formations.

Internal formations can also be seen as "fetters" or "knots" of suffering deep in our consciousness. The knots are created when we react emotionally to what others say and do, and also when we repeatedly suppress our awareness of both pleasant and unpleasant feelings and thoughts. The fetters that bind us can be identified as any painful feeling or pleasant feeling that has become addictive, such as anger, hatred, pride, doubt, sorrow, or attachment. They are forged by confusion and a lack of understanding, by our misperceptions regarding our selves and reality.

By practicing mindfulness, we are able to recognize and transform unpleasant feelings and emotions as soon as they arise, so they do not become fetters. When we do not let ourselves react to the words and actions of others, when we are able to keep our minds calm and peaceful, internal formations are not formed, and we experience greater happiness and joy. Our families, friends, and associates will also benefit from our greater understanding and love.

In our consciousness, there are also the seeds of happiness, such as joy, freedom, calm, and the ability to let go, to forgive, and to love. But these seeds need water every day or they will never thrive. When we are able to nourish these seeds with mindfulness, they will sprout and offer us the flowers and fruits of happiness. This is the object of the latter part of the exercise.

This exercise does not need to be practiced all at one time. It can be divided into several shorter exercises to be practiced over a longer period of time, say, three to six months.

EXERCISE 8

Looking Deeply into Anger to Transform It

---

1. Breathing in, I contemplate an angry person.   *angry person*

    Breathing out, I see the suffering of that person.   *suffering*

2. Breathing in, I see the damage done by anger to myself and others.   *damage done by anger*

    Breathing out, I see that anger burns and destroys everything.   *anger burns and destroys*

3. Breathing in, I see roots of anger in   *roots in my body*
    my body.

    Breathing out, I see roots of anger   *roots in my*
    in my consciousness.   *consciousness*

4. Breathing in, I see the roots of anger   *roots in pride*
    in pride and ignorance.   *and ignorance*

    Breathing out, I smile to my pride   *I smile*
    and ignorance.

5. Breathing in, I see how the angry   *angry person*
    person suffers.   *suffers*

    Breathing out, I know that person   *needs compassion*
    needs my compassion.

6. Breathing in, I see the environment   *Their*
    and the suffering of the angry person.   *environment*
                                                 and suffering

    Breathing out, I understand their   *I understand*
    environment and suffering.

7. Breathing in, I see how I burn myself   *burning myself*
    with the fire of anger.   *with anger*

    Breathing out, I feel compassion for   *feeling*
    myself burning with anger.   *compassion*

8. Breathing in, I know my anger makes   *anger makes*
    me look ugly.   *me ugly*

    Breathing out, I know I am the cause   *I cause my*
    of this ugliness.   *ugliness*

9. Breathing in, I see when angry I am like a burning house.

    Breathing out, I go back to myself to put out the fire.

    myself a burning house

    come back to put out the fire

10. Breathing in, I vow to help the other suffer less.

    Breathing out, I see I am able to help them suffer less.

    vow to help the other

    able to help

This is an exercise to help us face anger in ourselves and in others.

The Buddha taught that the fire of anger can burn up everything we have done to bring happiness to ourselves and others. There is not one of us who does not have seeds of anger in their heart, and if those seeds are daily watered, they will grow rapidly and cause us and those around us to suffer.

When we are angry, we should come back to ourselves by means of our conscious breathing. We should not look at or listen to the one we feel is making us angry and causing us to suffer. In fact, the main root of our suffering is the seed of anger in us. The other person may have said or done something out of lack of skill or mindfulness, or as a result of their own suffering. Someone who is suffering too much generally spills their suffering onto others. They need our help, not our anger. We come to see this when we come back to our breathing to take care of our anger.

Buddha says that anger makes us look ugly. If we are able to breathe when we are angry and recognize the ugliness anger brings with it, that recognition acts as a bell of mindfulness. We breathe and smile mindfully in order to bring some calm into our hearts, at the same time relaxing the nervous system and the tense muscles of our face. We can continue breathing mindfully as we practice walking meditation in the open air, looking deeply at what has happened. Mindfulness and conscious breathing are sources of energy and can calm the storm of anger, which itself is also a source of energy. If we keep on practicing mindfulness in order to take care of our anger with the affection of a mother when she takes her small child in her arms, then not only shall we calm the storm but we shall also be able to find out where our anger really comes from. This insight will transform our anger, and when the practice is ripe enough, it will transform the root of anger in us.[4]

EXERCISE 9

Contemplating My Daily Consumption of the Four Nutriments

1. Breathing in, I am aware of the edible food I consume every day.

   everyday consumption of edible food

   Breathing out, I see the effect of my consumption on my life.

   effect on my life

2. Breathing in, I am aware of the effect of my consumption on the universe.

   effect of consumption on the universe

   Breathing out, I am determined to eat in a way that reduces the suffering of beings.

   determined to reduce suffering

3. Breathing in, I am aware of the sense impressions I consume every day.

   aware of sense impressions

   Breathing out, I am aware of their effect on my emotional state.

   aware of effect on emotional state

4. For more about this subject, see Thich Nhat Hanh, *Anger: Wisdom for Cooling the Flames* (Berkeley, CA: Parallax Press, 2002).

4. Breathing in, I am aware that what I consume through my senses has an effect on society.   *effect of consumption on society*

 Breathing out, I am determined to choose carefully what sense impressions I consume.   *choosing sense impressions carefully*

5. Breathing in, I am aware of the desires and aspirations I consume every day.   *everyday desires and aspirations*

 Breathing out, I see their effect on my life.   *effect on my life*

6. Breathing in, I am aware of the effect of my desires and aspirations on society.   *effect on society*

 Breathing out, I am determined to base them on understanding and love.   *determined to base on understanding and love*

7. Breathing in, I am aware of the collective consciousness that nourishes me every day.   *collective consciousness*

 Breathing out, I am aware that the collective is made of the individual.   *collective made of individual*

8. Breathing in, I am determined to protect myself from the negative aspects of collective consciousness.   *protecting myself from negative aspects*

 Breathing out, I am determined to contribute positively to collective consciousness.   *contributing positively*

When you receive the Five Mindfulness Trainings,[5] you resolve to follow the direction of right consumption for body and mind. You are aware that a proper diet is crucial for self-transformation and the transformation of society. This exercise is based on the Sutra of the Four Nutriments. According to this sutra, there are four ways in which beings consume: edible food, sense contacts, intentions and desires, and collective consciousness.

The practice of mindful consumption is crucial for our own well-being and for the well-being of our planet. If we continue to consume in a thoughtless way, there will be no future for ourselves, our children, and our grandchildren.

Our consumption of edible food necessarily involves some suffering for other beings. If we enjoy a vegan diet, the suffering is less. A diet that includes meat and other products of factory farming not only causes suffering to the animals; it also causes deforestation and significantly reduces the availability of arable land for the growth of crops for human consumption. Methane (the gas produced in part by decomposing organic matter) contributes more to the production of greenhouse gases than cars do. We can experience joy when we know that we are reducing the suffering of beings by the way we eat.

When the sense organs—eyes, ears, nose, tongue, body, and mind—are in touch with the sense objects—forms, sounds, scents, tastes, and mental objects—the energy we receive can be wholesome or unwholesome. Mindfulness tells us what kinds of sense contact to avoid and what kinds to foster: what films to watch, what music to listen to, what books to read, what conversations to follow, what thoughts to nurture.

When we have an intention or desire, it can give us so much energy. If our desire is the mind of love that wants to reduce the suffering of beings, we bring happiness to ourselves and our loved ones. If we want power, fame, or sensual gratification, we can cause suffering to our loved ones and ourselves.

5. Please see appendix, p. 173.

Our consciousness is inevitably influenced by the collective consciousness that contains strong seeds of fear and discrimination. If we are not careful, we can consume the collective fear. The collective consciousness also has many beautiful aspects that have been nourished by spiritual practice for thousands of years. We know that we should enjoy the company of good spiritual friends in order to be nourished by the wholesome elements of collective consciousness.

As you meditate, you can look deeply at these forms of nutriment that play an important role in your physical and mental health.

EXERCISE 10

Seeing the Five Mindfulness Trainings as a Way Out of Suffering

1. Breathing in, I am aware of the suffering brought about by the destruction of life.

   suffering brought about by destruction of life

   Breathing out, I give rise to compassion for the victims of violence.

   compassion for victims of violence

2. Breathing in, I am determined not to kill.

   determined not to kill

   Breathing out, I am determined to cultivate nonviolence in actions of body, speech, and mind.

   nonviolence in my actions

3. Breathing in, I am aware of the suffering *suffering from*
    brought about by stealing, exploitation, *stealing, exploi-*
    and social injustice. *tation, social*
    injustice

    Breathing out, I give rise to loving- *loving-kindness*
    kindness for the victims of social *for the victims*
    injustice.

4. Breathing in, I feel compassion *compassion*
    for victims of exploitation. *for victims of*
    exploitation

    Breathing out, I am determined to *living simply and*
    live simply, grateful for the conditions *gratefully*
    of happiness I already have.

5. Breathing in, I am aware of suffering *suffering caused*
    brought about by sexual misconduct. *by sexual*
    misconduct

    Breathing out, I feel compassion for *compassion for*
    victims of sexual misconduct. *victims*

6. Breathing in, I am aware of harm *harm to children*
    done to children and young people *and young people*
    by irresponsible sexual behavior.

    Breathing out, I am determined to *determined to*
    learn to take care of my sexual energy. *take care of my*
    sexual energy

7. Breathing in, I am aware of the *suffering caused*
    suffering brought about by unmindful *by unmindful*
    speech. *speech*

    Breathing out, I give rise to loving *loving thoughts*
    thoughts and mindful words in my *and mindful*
    heart. *words*

8. Breathing in, I feel compassion for the one I have hurt by my words. *compassion for one I have hurt*

Breathing out, I am determined to listen deeply and speak mindfully. *listening deeply speaking mindfully*

9. Breathing in, I am aware of the suffering brought about by unmindful consumption. *suffering due to unmindful consumption*

Breathing out, I aspire to protect my body and mind. *protecting body and mind*

10. Breathing in, I feel compassion for someone who is addicted. *compassion for someone addicted*

Breathing out, I am determined to abstain from alcohol, drugs, electronic games, and other toxic products for the rest of my life. *determined to abstain from toxic products*

11. Breathing in, I see how the Five Mindfulness Trainings protect me, others, and all species. *mindfulness trainings protect*

Breathing out, I am determined to practice them for my whole life. *determined to practice them*

12. Breathing in, I see myself practicing the mindfulness trainings with the sangha. *practicing the trainings with the sangha*

Breathing out, I feel happy to be practicing the trainings with the sangha's support. *happy to be practicing with the sangha's support*

The Five Mindfulness Trainings are not prohibitions to restrict our freedom. They are not sanctions we have to obey. They are the practice of true love that brings happiness, both to the one who practices them and to many others. The mindfulness trainings are the fruit of our mindfulness and experience. They are the practice of Applied Buddhism, protecting us as well as those with whom we share our lives. This guided meditation waters the seed of compassion in us by helping us become aware of the suffering we cause ourselves and others when we do not follow the guidelines of the Five Mindfulness Trainings.

Thanks to mindfulness, we see how the mindfulness trainings preserve our freedom and happiness now and for days to come. We receive and practice the mindfulness trainings because we see how they help us. We follow them in order to preserve our inner freedom. They help us not to fall into the traps that make us suffer. Buddha means being mindful. Since these trainings are the fruit of the concrete practice of mindfulness, they are the Buddha. They are the embodiment of the Dharma, which is the path shown by the Buddha. They are also the embodiment of the sangha, the community of all those who have taken up the path of practice. The sangha is present in and around us. When we practice the trainings, we are protected by the Buddha, the Dharma, and the sangha. These Three Jewels are always present in the Five Mindfulness Trainings. Therefore, to practice the Five Mindfulness Trainings is to take refuge in the Three Jewels. The trainings nourish confidence and enlightenment in the practitioner. We recite the mindfulness trainings in order to remember their teachings and to look deeply at the benefits of being guided by them.

In this exercise, certain concrete examples of suffering are given so that we can give rise to compassion. To help keep our meditation practice alive and more relevant, we can substitute examples from our own life in our meditation. For a more detailed meditation in mindful consumption (the fifth mindfulness training), see the preceding exercise.

EXERCISE 11

Healing Past Wounds and Beginning Anew

---

1. Breathing in, I visualize some damage   *damage in*
   I have done in the past.   *the past*

   Breathing out, I see the suffering I   *suffering I caused*
   caused in the past.

2. Breathing in, I seeing my lack of   *lack of*
   understanding in the past.   *understanding*

   Breathing out, I see my lack of   *lack of*
   mindfulness in the past.   *mindfulness*

3. Breathing in, I see the past present   *past present*
   in me now.   *in me*

   Breathing out, I see the wounds of the   *past wounds*
   past present in me now.   *present in me*

4. Breathing in, I see the past present in   *past present in*
   the other now.   *the other*

   Breathing out, I see the wounds of the   *past wounds*
   past present in the other now.   *present in the*
                                                  other

5. Breathing in, I say I am sorry and   *I am sorry*
   am determined to begin anew.

   Breathing out, I vow not to do it again.   *vow not to do*
                                                  it again

6. Breathing in, I see that the Five Mindfulness Trainings are a protection for me and the other.

   mindfulness trainings protect

   Breathing out, I am determined to practice the mindfulness trainings deeply.

   determined to practice

7. Breathing in, I know that by transforming the present, I transform the past.

   transforming the present, I transform the past

   Breathing out, I know I have to live mindfully and with understanding in the present.

   vowing to live mindfully in the present

8. Breathing in, I smile to the present.

   smiling to the present

   Breathing out, I am determined to take good care of the present.

   taking care of the present

9. Breathing in, I transform the past by my present action.

   transforming the past

   Breathing out, I see my present action leading to a better future.

   present action, better future

The purpose of this exercise is to enable us to let go and begin life anew. All of us have made mistakes, have harmed or wounded ourselves and others, especially those who are close to us.

Often we ourselves have been wounded—by our parents, by our society, by those we have vowed to love. But we know also that because of our lack of understanding and mindfulness, we have—to a greater or lesser extent—wounded ourselves and others. Moreover, because we lack understanding and mindfulness, we have not been able to transform the wounds that we bear deep within. Above all else, this exercise helps us to accept our wounds and to recognize the ones that we are responsible for. When we can acknowledge our responsibility, we will not blame others but will instead feel compassion and begin anew.

The past has not been lost; it has become the present. If we are able to be in touch with the present, we are able to be in touch with the past; if we know how to be responsible for and transform the present, we can transform the past. The Five Mindfulness Trainings are not laws to coerce us but the fruit of mindfulness and an awakened mind. Their role is to protect us and guarantee our own peace and the peace of others. With the mindfulness trainings as a foundation, even on the same day, we are able to bring joy to others and relieve them of their suffering.

CHAPTER 3

The Objects of Mind

In the Anapanasati Sutta, the section on objects of mind has four components: fading of desire, impermanence, the ending of dualistic conceptions (such as birth-death, coming-going), and letting go. These ways of understanding are essential for our realization of enlightenment and liberation. However, intellectual understanding is not enough. Our mindfulness and meditation need to be sustained and wholehearted for us to realize true liberation. The following exercises are to help us in this.

The first eighteen exercises in this chapter have been developed based on the last four of the sixteen exercises taught by the Buddha in the Anapanasati Sutta.

EXERCISE 1

The Impermanent Nature of Myself and All Things

---

1. Breathing in, I am aware of the hair on my head.   *hair*

   Breathing out, I see the impermanence of the hair on my head.   *impermanent*

2. Breathing in, I am aware of my eyes.   *eyes*

    Breathing out, I see the impermanence   *impermanent*
    of my eyes.

3. Breathing in, I am aware of my ears.   *ears*

    Breathing out, I see the impermanence   *impermanent*
    of my ears.

4. Breathing in, I am aware of my nose.   *nose*

    Breathing out, I see the impermanence   *impermanent*
    of my nose.

5. Breathing in, I am aware of my tongue.   *tongue*

    Breathing out, I see the impermanence   *impermanent*
    of my tongue.

6. Breathing in, I am aware of my heart.   *heart*

    Breathing out, I see the impermanence   *impermanent*
    of my heart.

7. Breathing in, I am aware of my liver.   *liver*

    Breathing out, I see the impermanence   *impermanent*
    of my liver.

8. Breathing in, I am aware of my lungs.   *lungs*

    Breathing out, I see the impermanence   *impermanent*
    of my lungs.

9. Breathing in, I am aware of my   *intestines*
    intestines.

    Breathing out, I see the impermanence   *impermanent*
    of my intestines.

10. Breathing in, I am aware of my kidneys.   *kidneys*

    Breathing out, I see the impermanence   *impermanent*
    of my kidneys.

11. Breathing in, I am aware of my body.   *body*

    Breathing out, I see the impermanence   *impermanent*
    of my body.

12. Breathing in, I am aware of political   *political regimes*
    regimes.

    Breathing out, I see the impermanence   *impermanent*
    of political regimes.

13. Breathing in, I am aware of my nation.   *nation*

    Breathing out, I see the impermanence   *impermanent*
    of my nation.

14. Breathing in, I am aware of the human   *human species*
    species.

    Breathing out, I see the impermanence   *impermanent*
    of the human species.

15. Breathing in, I am aware of the planet   *planet earth*
    earth.

    Breathing out, I see the impermanence   *impermanent*
    of the planet earth.

This exercise helps us to acknowledge the impermanent nature of everything. Acknowledging impermanence in mindfulness leads us to a deeper view of what life is. It is very important to understand that impermanence is not a negative aspect of life. Impermanence is the very basis of life. If what exists were not impermanent, no life could continue. If a seed of corn were not impermanent, it could not become a corn plant. If a tiny child were not impermanent, she could not grow into an adult.

Life is impermanent, but that does not mean it is not worth living. It is precisely because we are aware of the impermanent nature of everything that we cherish life in the present moment. We know how to live each moment deeply and use it in a responsible way. If we are able to live the present moment completely, we will not feel regret later. We will know how to care for those who are close to us and how to bring them happiness today. When we accept that all things are impermanent, we will not be incapacitated by suffering when things decay and die. We can remain peaceful and content in the face of any change, whether it results in prosperity or decline, success or failure.

Many people are always restless and in a hurry and do not know how to look after their bodies and minds. Night and day, little by little, they barter their health away in order to obtain material comforts. In the end, they destroy body and mind for the sake of these things that ultimately are not of the greatest importance. This exercise can also help us look after our bodies and minds.

In our own time, the reality of climate change is forcing us to look deeply to see that even our planet Earth and all the species that live on it are impermanent. When people see the life of our planet endangered by climate change, many of them fall into a state of despair. In such a state, they cannot do anything to help the situation, and they may well die of despair before they die as a result of climate change. In order to transform this despair, they need to accept the fact that all civilizations are impermanent. Only then will they have enough inner peace to be able to act wisely and impact their contribution to climate change. It is the same in the case of sickness or disability: once a person can accept that she is sick and may die as a result, she can live at peace in a way that can actually prolong her life.

EXERCISE 2
Contemplating My Own Impermanence

1. Breathing in, I know I will grow old. *I will grow old*

   Breathing out, I know I shall not always *not always young*
   be young and healthy. *and healthy*

2. Breathing in, I know I will fall sick. *falling sick*

   Breathing out, I know I can't escape *no escape*
   sickness.

3. Breathing in, I know I will die. *I will die*

   Breathing out, I know I can't escape *no escape*
   death.

4. Breathing in, I know that one day I *abandon all*
   will have to abandon all that I cherish *I cherish*
   today.

   Breathing out, I know I can't hold on *can't hold on*
   forever to all that I cherish. *forever*

5. Breathing in, I know that my actions   *actions only*
    are the only belongings I can take with   *belongings*
    me.

    Breathing out, I know I cannot escape   *cannot escape*
    the consequences of my actions.   *the consequences*

6. Breathing in, I am determined to live   *live in*
    my days deeply in mindfulness.   *mindfulness*

    Breathing out, I see the peace and joy of   *the peace and joy*
    living mindfully.

7. Breathing in, I vow to offer joy each day   *offer joy to*
    to my beloved.   *beloved*

    Breathing out, I vow each day to ease   *ease pain of*
    the pain of my beloved.   *beloved*

This exercise helps us to come face-to-face with the anxieties and fears that lie deep in our subconscious, and to transform these latent tendencies (called *anuśaya*). In principle, we all know very well that we cannot avoid growing old, falling sick, dying, or being separated from those we love, but we do not want to give our attention to these things. We do not want to be in touch with the anxiety and the fear, but prefer to let them sleep deep in our minds. That is why they are called latent tendencies (*anuśaya* literally means "lying asleep along with"). But although they are lying asleep, they still follow us and unconsciously influence our way of thinking, speaking, and acting. When we hear people speaking about, or are ourselves witness to, old age, sickness, death, and separation from loved ones, the latent tendencies in us are watered and become more deeply rooted. Along with our other sorrows, longings, hatreds, and anger, these unresolved blocks of anxiety and fear become stronger. Because we are not able to resolve them, we repress them, and this causes mental and physical illnesses whose symptoms can be recognized in our actions, thoughts, and words. We must learn a different way to treat the *anuśaya*. The Buddha himself taught this exercise and advised his followers to practice it every day. Buddha taught that rather than repressing our fears and anxieties, we should invite them into our consciousness, to recognize and smile to them.

When we begin to practice conscious breathing, mindfulness is lit up within us. When the fears and anxieties arise, we bathe them in that light of mindfulness. We only need to acknowledge the presence of our fears and smile to them as we would smile to an old friend. Then, quite naturally, they will lose some of their energy. When, once again, they return to our subconscious, they will be that much weaker. If we practice every day, they will continue to grow weaker. There will be good circulation in our consciousness that will resolve stagnation, and the symptoms of our physical or mental sickness will disappear. By recognizing and smiling to our fear and anxiety, we gradually see into their essence. When our understanding of that essence is ripe, the latent tendencies will be transformed.

In our own time, people are very afraid that our civilization and even the human species will come to an end as a result of global warming. Because of this fear, they are not able to see clearly what they should or should not do. The first step is to accept that our species is impermanent, and that sooner or later, it has to end. However, it does not have to end by global warming, and the understanding of impermanence gives people enough peace and calm to act in a positive way.

This exercise helps us to live the present moment in a peaceful, happy, and awakened way. We will come to understand that we are able to bring joy to those around us right away.

EXERCISE 3

Looking Deeply into Sensual Pleasure and Their Objects in Order to Let Go

---

1. Breathing in, I contemplate the attractive body of a woman.   *a woman's attractive body*

   Breathing out, I see the impermanent nature of her body.   *impermanent*

2. Breathing in, I contemplate the attractive body of a man.   *a man's attractive body*

   Breathing out, I see the impermanent nature of his body.   *impermanent*

3. Breathing in, I contemplate the danger that my craving sex can bring about.   *danger of craving sex*

   Breathing out, I contemplate letting go.   *letting go*

4. Breathing in, I contemplate the hardships my craving sex can bring about.   *hardships from craving sex*

   Breathing out, I contemplate letting go.   *letting go*

5. Breathing in, I contemplate the complications that my craving sex can bring about. *complications from craving sex*

   Breathing out, I contemplate letting go.   *letting go*

6. Breathing in, I contemplate running after my desire for possessions.   *running after possessions*

   Breathing out, I see the impermanent nature of riches and possessions.   *possessions impermanent*

7. Breathing in, I contemplate running   *desire for a car*
    after my desire for a new car.

    Breathing out, I see the impermanent   *cars impermanent*
    nature of cars.

8. Breathing in, I contemplate running   *desire for a house*
    after my desire for a house.

    Breathing out, I see the impermanent   *houses*
    nature of houses.   *impermanent*

9. Breathing in, I contemplate running   *desire to be*
    after my desire for being fashionable.   *fashionable*

    Breathing out, I see the impermanent   *fashion*
    nature of all fashions.   *impermanent*

10. Breathing in, I contemplate the   *danger from*
    danger that seeking possessions brings   *seeking*
    about.   *possessions*

    Breathing out, I contemplate letting go. *letting go*

11. Breathing in, I contemplate the hard-   *hardships*
    ships that seeking possessions brings   *from seeking*
    about.   *possessions*

    Breathing out, I contemplate letting go. *letting go*

12. Breathing in, I contemplate the   *complications*
    complications that seeking possessions   *from seeking*
    brings about.   *possessions*

    Breathing out, I contemplate letting go. *letting go*

13. Breathing in, I contemplate the pursuit   *pursuit of fame*
    of fame.

    Breathing out, I see that fame is   *fame*
    impermanent and fragile.   *impermanent*

14. Breathing in, I contemplate the danger   *danger of pursu-*
    of pursuing fame.   *ing fame*

    Breathing out, I contemplate letting go.   *letting go*

15. Breathing in, I contemplate the hard-   *hardships from*
    ships from pursuing fame.   *pursuing fame*

    Breathing out, I contemplate letting go.   *letting go*

16. Breathing in, I contemplate the   *complications of*
    complications pursuing fame can   *pursuing fame*
    bring about.

    Breathing out, I contemplate letting go.   *letting go*

17. Breathing in, I contemplate my desire   *fine food and*
    to eat fine food and wear fine clothes.   *clothes*

    Breathing out, I see the vain and   *impermanent*
    impermanent nature of fine clothes
    and food.

18. Breathing in, I contemplate the danger   *danger of fine food*
    of my desire for fine clothes and food.   *and clothes*

    Breathing out, I contemplate letting go.   *letting go*

19. Breathing in, I contemplate the hardships caused by my desire for fine food and clothes.   *hardships from fine food and clothes*

    Breathing out, I contemplate letting go.   *letting go*

20. Breathing in, I contemplate the complications from my desire for fine food and clothes.   *complications from fine food and clothes*

    Breathing out, I contemplate letting go.   *letting go*

21. Breathing in, I contemplate an indolent and indulgent way of life.   *indolent and indulgent*

    Breathing out, I see the danger of an indolent and indulgent way of life.   *danger*

22. Breathing in, I contemplate letting go.   *letting go*

    Breathing out, I contemplate letting go.   *letting go*

This exercise helps us to see the impermanence, as well as the dangers, complications, and hardships, of our endless pursuit of fame and material and sensual pleasure. We go through countless agonies, complications, and dangers large and small in order to enjoy these sensual pleasures. We could waste our whole lives chasing after them without there being any guarantee of satisfaction. Even if we did attain them, we would discover that they are not only short-lived but also dangerous for our health and the peace of our body and mind.

Real happiness cannot exist when we are not totally free. Burdened by so many ambitions, we lose our freedom. We are always grasping at something; there are so many things we want to do at the same time, and that is why we do not have the time to live. We think that all our projects are necessary for our happiness, and that if they are taken from us, we will suffer. However, if we look more closely, we shall see that the things at which we grasp, the things that keep us constantly busy, are in fact obstacles to our happiness. We know that true happiness is only possible with freedom, living in mindfulness, and practicing compassion.

The practice of this meditation exercise should be followed by the practice of exercises that help us to let go, like the two preceding ones.

EXERCISE 4
Non-Self

1. Breathing in, I am aware of my body.   *my body*

   Breathing out, I smile to my body.   *I smile*

2. Breathing in, I am aware this body is not I.   *body not I*

   Breathing out, I am aware I do not own this body.   *I do not own it*

3. Breathing in, I am aware of a feeling.   *a feeling*

   Breathing out, I smile to this feeling.   *I smile*

4. Breathing in, I am aware this feeling is not I.   *feeling not I*

   Breathing out, I am aware I do not own this feeling.   *I do not own it*

5. Breathing in, I am aware of a   *a perception*
    perception.

    Breathing out, I smile to this   *I smile*
    perception.

6. Breathing in, I am aware this   *perception not I*
    perception is not I.

    Breathing out, I am aware I do not   *I do not own it*
    own this perception.

7. Breathing in, I am aware of a mental   *a mental*
    formation.   *formation*

    Breathing out, I smile to this mental   *I smile*
    formation.

8. Breathing in, I am aware this mental   *mental formation*
    formation is not I.   *not I*

    Breathing out, I am aware I do not   *I do not own it*
    own this mental formation.

9. Breathing in, I am aware of   *consciousness*
    consciousness.

    Breathing out, I smile to consciousness.   *I smile*

10. Breathing in, I am aware that   *consciousness*
    consciousness is not I.   *not I*

    Breathing out, I am aware I do not own   *I do not own it*
    consciousness.

11. Breathing in, I knowing I am not limited by these five aggregates.	*not limited by five aggregates*
Breathing out, I know these five aggregates are not limited by me.	*five aggregates not limited by me*
12. Breathing in, I know this body is not born, does not die.	*body not born, not dying*
Breathing out, I know that I also am not born, do not die.	*I not born not dying*
13. Breathing in, I smile to this birthless and deathless body.	*I smile to this birthless, deathless body*
Breathing out, I smile to this birthless and deathless self.	*I smile to this birthless, deathless self*

This exercise trains us to look deeply at the nature of selflessness. The body and the other bases of perception (eyes, ears, nose, tongue, and mind) are not myself. Nor do they belong to a myself that lies outside the six sense organs and the five aggregates.

The five aggregates are the body, feelings, perceptions, mental formations, and consciousness. These five aggregates are not myself, and they are also not owned by a self that exists apart from them. According to the normal definition, myself (the self) is a permanent entity existing independently from so-called non-self entities. Buddhism teaches that there is no such self because, in reality, there is nothing changeless that can exist independently of all else. What, then, is the meaning of the words "I" and "self" in this exercise, and to what do they refer? The "I" here refers to the person who is meditating, who is a compound of the five aggregates. The five aggregates are themselves a river of constantly transforming phenomena, which are not separate entities. If we understand that, then there is nothing wrong with the use of the word "I." If we are clearly aware that self is made of non-self elements, we can use the expression "self" without fear—like Buddha when he asked Ananda: "Do *you* wish to come to Vulture Peak with *me*?"

The wrong views of self can be enumerated as follows:

1. The body is the self (I am this body, *Satkāyadrsti*).

2. The body is not the self, but it belongs to the self (this body belongs to me).

3. The body is in the self, and the self is in the body (even though the body is not the self, it is in the self; even though the self is not the body, it is in the body).

4. The body is not the self, but it is also not something independent of the self.

5. The universe is the self and the self is the universe (the self is eternal as is the universe because the self is the universe).

It is important to remember that we meditate on no-self in order to uproot the idea of a permanent and changeless self, not to establish a theory of eternalism or nihilism. Eternalism (*sassata-ditthi* in Pali) and nihilism (*uccheda-ditthi* in Pali) are both wrong views, traps that the Buddha taught his disciples to avoid. They are the foundation of all wrong views. If we are able to go beyond these two extremes, we can freely use the word "I," just as the Buddha did with the understanding, "This body is not me," or "I am not this body."

The world and the cosmos are impermanent and subject to birth and death. To identify self with the world or the cosmos is also a confused notion if it means we are caught in "eternalist" or nihilistic thinking: "I am the universe. As long as the universe is there, I continue to exist. When the universe ceases to exist, I cease to exist." This is not so, for reality is birthless and deathless, without self and without other, without coming and going. It is only by realizing this reality that we can transcend the wrong view of self. Those who simply repeat over and over again "no self" as a religious doctrine have probably lost their way and entered the view of nihilism.

EXERCISE 5
The Interdependence and Non-Duality of All That Is

---

1. Breathing in, I am in touch with the flower.   *flower*

   Breathing out, I am in touch with its fragrance and beauty.   *fragrance and beauty*

2. Breathing in, I am in touch with the sun in the flower.   *sun in flower*

   Breathing out, I know that without the sun there would be no flower.   *without sun, no flower*

3. Breathing in, I am in touch with the cloud in the flower.   *cloud in flower*

   Breathing out, I know that without the cloud there would be no flower. *without cloud, no flower*

4. Breathing in, I am in touch with the earth in the flower.

   earth in flower

   Breathing out, I know that without the earth there would be no flower.

   without earth, no flower

5. Breathing in, I am in touch with the air in the flower.

   air in flower

   Breathing out, I know that without the air there would be no flower.

   without air, no flower

6. Breathing in, I am in touch with space in the flower.

   space in flower

   Breathing out, I know that without space there would be no flower.

   without space, no flower

7. Breathing in, I am in touch with consciousness in the flower.

   consciousness in flower

   Breathing out, I know that without consciousness there would be no flower.

   without consciousness no flower

8. Breathing in, I know that the flower manifests from the six elements.

   flower from six elements

   Breathing out, I smile to the six elements in the flower.

   I smile

9. Breathing in, I see the impermanence of the flower.

   flower impermanent

   Breathing out, I see the flower becoming compost.

   becoming compost

10. Breathing in, I am in touch with   *compost*
    the compost.

    Breathing out, I am in touch with   *impurity and smell*
    the impurity and smell of compost.

11. Breathing in, I am in touch with   *compost from*
    the compost manifesting from the   *six elements*
    six elements.

    Breathing out, I smile to the six   *I smile*
    elements in the compost.

12. Breathing in, I see the impermanence   *compost*
    of compost.   *impermanent*

    Breathing out, I see the compost   *becoming flower*
    becoming a flower.

13. Breathing in, I am in touch with   *cloud in compost*
    the cloud in the compost.

    Breathing out, I know that without   *without cloud, no*
    the cloud there is no compost.   *compost*

14. Breathing in, I am in touch with the   *earth in compost*
    earth in the compost.

    Breathing out, I know that without   *without earth,*
    earth there is no compost.   *no compost*

15. Breathing in, I am in touch with the air in the compost.

    air in compost

    Breathing out, I know that without air there is no compost.

    without air, no compost

16. Breathing in, I am in touch with space in the compost.

    space in compost

    Breathing out, I know that without space there is no compost.

    without space, no compost

17. Breathing in, I am in touch with consciousness in the compost.

    consciousness in compost

    Breathing out, I know that without consciousness there is no compost.

    without consciousness no compost

This exercise helps us see the interdependent arising and nonduality of all that is. This insight liberates us from all wrong perceptions, all fear, and all anxiety. It breaks through all the barriers that are created by our perceptions, which come from the habits of thinking and discriminating in a dualistic way. The barriers between birth and death, being and nonbeing, purity and defilement are no longer there, and the meditator lives without fear and in the vast space of freedom. The teaching on interdependent arising is described in the Avatamsaka Sutra as interbeing and interpenetration. This exercise helps us to see the one in the all, and the all in the one. Nonduality means that there are not two, but it does not mean that there is only one.

EXERCISE 6

Contemplating Wrong Perceptions That Are Based on Being Caught in Signs

1. Breathing in, I am aware of myself   *myself as five*
    as a collection of five aggregates.   *aggregates*

    Breathing out, I see this collection   *five aggregates*
    of five aggregates rooted and based   *in all that is*
    in all that is.

2. Breathing in, I am aware of myself   *myself made of*
    as made up of what is not myself   *what is not myself*
    (warmth, water, air, earth, ancestors,
    habits, society, economy).

    Breathing out, I see that my perception   *perception of*
    of myself is often wrong.   *myself often*
                                               wrong

3. Breathing in, I am aware of the   *humans an*
    human species as an animal species   *animal species*
    with a culture that has made it
    dominant on earth.

    Breathing out, I see that the human   *not able to*
    species cannot exist without the   *exist without*
    animal, plant, and mineral species.   *other species*

4. Breathing in, I see the presence of the   *humans in other*
    human species in the animal, plant, and   *species*
    mineral species.

    Breathing out, I see that my idea of   *humans not an*
    humans as an independent species is   *independent*
    wrong.   *species*

5. Breathing in, I am aware that all animal   *animals have*
    species are born, die, and have feelings   *feelings and*
    and consciousness.   *consciousness*

    Breathing out, I see that the animal   *not able to*
    species cannot exist without the plants   *exist without*
    and minerals, the sun, the water, and   *other species*
    the air.

6. Breathing in, I see the presence of the   *animals in*
    animals in non-sentient beings; like   *non-sentient*
    plants, minerals, sun, water, and air.   *beings*

    Breathing out, I see that my idea of   *wrong idea of*
    animals as an independent category   *animals*
    is wrong.

7. Breathing in, I am aware of my life   *life beginning with*
    beginning at my birth and ending with   *birth ending with*
    my death.   *death*

    Breathing out, I see myself present in   *forms of life before*
    many different forms before my birth   *birth and after*
    and after I die (in the sun, water, air,   *death.*
    earth, ancestors, descendants, habits,
    society, economy).

8. Breathing in, I see that my life span   *unlimited life span*
    is not limited by my birth and death.

    Breathing out, I see that my notion   *life span a wrong*
    of a life span is wrong.   *notion*

This exercise originates in the Vajracchedika Prajñāpāramitā Sutra (in English, the Diamond Sutra), whose purpose is to help us break through four objects of our perception, which are called signs. These signs are like boxes that our perception uses to divide reality. The four signs are:

1. The sign of myself as a separately existing entity (parts 1 and 2)

2. The sign of the human species as a separately existing species (parts 3 and 4)

3. The sign of animal species as separately existing (parts 5 and 6)

4. The sign of a life span beginning with birth and ending in death (parts 7 and 8)

The quintessential Buddhist teaching is the teaching on emptiness (in Sanskrit, *śūnyatā*). Emptiness is a way of expressing that everything has the nature of interbeing and interpenetration. Our meditation practice of looking deeply breaks down the barriers between us and what seems to be other: the human species and all the other species, the animal species and the so-called non-sentient species, a short life span limited by space and time and a life span not limited in that way. If we are able to remove these four notions called signs, we will transcend all the limitations of our perceptions and transcend birth and death. We will realize fearlessness and be able to love all species as we love ourselves. We shall practice to protect all species, whether plant, animal, or mineral. Anyone who works to protect the plants, the animals, the environment, and our earth, can take the Vajracchedika Sutra as a guide for their activism.

Activism based on this vision will never come from anger, discontent, or despair. Activism founded in the removal of these four signs only takes understanding and love as its substance. The person who acts in this way is happy and at peace while engaging in activism.

EXERCISE 7

Taking Care of the Wounded Child in Myself and My Parents

---

1. Breathing in, I see myself as a five-year-old child. *myself at five years*

   Breathing out, I smile to the five-year-old child. *I smile*

2. Breathing in, I see the five-year-old as fragile and vulnerable. *five-year-old fragile*

   Breathing out, I smile with compassion to the five-year-old in me. *smile with compassion*

3. Breathing in, I listen to the five-year-old crying in me. *five-year-old crying*

   Breathing out, I embrace the child in me with understanding. *embrace with understanding*

4. Breathing in, I see my father as a five-year-old boy. *father five years old*

   Breathing out, I smile to my father as a five-year-old boy. *I smile*

5. Breathing in, I see my five-year-old father as fragile and vulnerable. *five-year-old father fragile*

   Breathing out, I smile with compassion and understanding. *smile with compassion*

6. Breathing in, I see my father suffering as a child.

   Breathing out, I see the wounded child still present in my father.

   father suffering as a child

   wounded child in him still present

7. Breathing in, I see my father in myself.

   Breathing out, I see my father's wounded child in myself.

   father in me

   father's wounded child in me

8. Breathing in, I see my mother as a five-year-old girl.

   Breathing out, I smile to my mother at five years old.

   mother five years old

   I smile

9. Breathing in, I see my five-year-old mother as fragile and vulnerable.

   Breathing out, I smile with compassion and understanding.

   five-year-old mother fragile

   smile with compassion

10. Breathing in, I see my mother suffering as a child.

    Breathing out, I see the wounded child still present in my mother.

    mother suffering as a child

    wounded child in her still present

11. Breathing in, I seeing my mother in me.

    Breathing out, I see my mother's wounded child in myself.

    mother in me

    mother's wounded child in me

12. Breathing in, my father in me is
    breathing.

    Breathing out, my mother in me
    is breathing.

    *father breathing
    in me*

    *mother breathing
    in me*

13. Breathing in, I understand the
    difficulties of my father in myself.

    Breathing out, I vow to transform
    them for my father and myself.

    *difficulties of father
    in me*

    *vow to transform
    for father and me*

14. Breathing in, I understand the
    difficulties of my mother in myself.

    Breathing out, I vow to transform
    them for my mother and myself.

    *difficulties of
    mother in me*

    *vow to transform
    for mother and me*

There are many ways we can apply the teachings of non-self in our daily lives. One of the easiest and most effective ways to do this is to see our parents and ancestors as non-self elements in what we call "myself." "Myself" is nothing more than a name for a whole lineage that we represent. The truth of no-self is fully confirmed by scientific discoveries in the realm of genetics. In spite of this scientific truth, it is not always easy for us to see that we are our parents. Some of us do not want to have anything to do with our parents. The fact is that if we cannot feel love and compassion for our parents, we cannot love ourselves.

This exercise has helped many young people reestablish happy and stable relations with their parents. At the same time, it has helped them transform accumulated resentment and even hatred that began to grow in them from a very young age.

There are people who cannot even think about their mothers

and fathers without feelings of pain and animosity. There are always seeds of love in the hearts of parents and children. Still, it is often very difficult for them to accept each other because they do not know how to water those seeds and resolve the conflicts that, although minor in the beginning, have accumulated and developed over time.

For the first step of the exercise, the practitioner visualizes herself as a five-year-old child. At that age, we are so easily hurt. A severe glance or a threatening or reproachful word can wound us deeply and give us an inferiority complex. When father makes mother suffer or mother makes father suffer, or both of them make each other suffer, a seed of suffering is sown and watered in the heart of the child. If this happens repeatedly, the child will grow up with many knots of suffering in her heart and will blame one or both of her parents. When we see ourselves as vulnerable children, we learn to feel compassion for ourselves, and that compassion suffuses us. We smile at that child of five years old with a smile of compassion.

In the next stage of the meditation, the practitioner visualizes his mother or his father as a five-year-old child. Usually, we think of our fathers as strict and severe, hard-to-please adults who only know how to resolve a problem by using their authority. But we also know that before a father was an adult, he was a little boy, just as vulnerable, just as fragile as we ourselves were. We can see that little boy cringing, falling silent, and not daring to open his mouth to speak whenever his own father, our grandfather, fell into a rage. We see that our father as a small boy may have been the victim of the hot temper, scowling, and violence of his father. It is often helpful to seek out an old family photograph album to find out what our mothers or fathers looked like when they were young children.

In our sitting meditation, we can befriend the children who were our mothers and fathers and smile to them affectionately, aware of their fragility and their vulnerability. When the feeling of compassion fills our hearts, we know that our meditation is beginning to bear fruit.

When we truly see and understand their suffering, it is impossible not to accept and love them. The accumulated resentment toward our parents will gradually be transformed as we practice this exercise. With this understanding, we begin to accept. We may be able to use this understanding and love in order to go back to our parents and help them transform, too. We know that this is possible because our understanding and our feelings of compassion have helped us transform ourselves, and we have already become easier, more gentle, calm, and patient. Patience and calm are two signs of true love.

EXERCISE 8

Seeing My Parents in Me and Practicing with Them

1. Breathing in, my father is breathing in with me.

   father breathing with me

   Breathing out, my father is breathing out with me.

2. Breathing in, I am sitting with my father's back.

   sitting with father's back

   Breathing out, I am breathing with my father's lungs.

   breathing with father's lungs

3. Breathing in, I feel light and at ease.

   light and at ease

   Breathing out, Daddy, do you feel light and at ease?

   Daddy, light and at ease?

4. Breathing in, my mother is breathing   *mother breathing*
    in with me.   *with me*

    Breathing out, my mother is breathing
    out with me.

5. Breathing in, I am sitting with my   *sitting with*
    mother's back.   *mother's back*

    Breathing out, I am breathing with my   *breathing with*
    mother's lungs.   *mother's lungs*

6. Breathing in, I feel light and at ease.   *light and at ease*

    Breathing out, Mummy, do you feel   *Mummy, light*
    light and at ease?   *and at ease?*

There was a day when, in my sitting meditation, I said to my father, who had already passed away many years ago: "Father, we have succeeded." I meant that we had succeeded in realizing the stopping and peace that is the fruit of meditation. While my father was alive, he was a civil servant and hardly ever had the time to practice sitting meditation and feel the joy of stopping. Now as I sat in meditation, I saw that as I meditated, my father was also meditating.

In meditation, you realize that your parents are in every cell of your body. When your parents die, they continue to live in you and in others. If you never knew your parents, you can learn to look deeply into your five skandhas in order to discover your parents there. Feelings, emotions, and ways of perceiving the world come from your upbringing, education, society, and friends, but there are also vestiges of the feelings, emotions, and perceptions of your parents. Mindfulness of your feelings and mind in daily life helps you recognize these traces.

You may have an idea of your father and mother outside of you. When you meditate, as in the above exercises, you will also have an idea of your mother and father within you. These two different ways of perceiving your parents interact and influence each other. If your father and mother never had an opportunity to practice meditation in their daily life, now, in a new continuation, they can enjoy the lightness and ease that meditation brings. If your parents are still alive, you will see that they benefit from your practice of breathing with them.

EXERCISE 9

Contemplating the Non-Local and Boundless Nature of All Things

1. Breathing in, I am aware of myself picking up an autumn leaf.   *picking up an autumn leaf*

   Breathing out, I touch the wonderful interdependent nature of that leaf.   *interdependent nature of leaf*

2. Breathing in, I am aware of myself alive here and now.   *myself alive now*

   Breathing out, I touch the wonderful interdependent nature of life in me and around me.   *interdependent nature of life*

3. Breathing in, I am aware of the leaf returning to the earth and arising as a new leaf.   *leaf returns to earth, arises anew*

   Breathing out, I see the leaf in thousands of different forms of birth and death.   *leaf in thousands of different forms*

4. Breathing in, I am aware of myself as a
    wonderful, interdependent reality.

    *myself wonderfully
    interdependent*

    Breathing out, I see that I manifest
    in many different forms of birth and
    death.

    *I manifest in many
    different forms*

5. Breathing in, I see that the leaf is not
    born, does not die, but only appears
    to be born and die.

    *leaf appears to
    be born and die*

    Breathing out, I see that I am not born
    and do not die but only appear to.

    *I appear to be
    born and die*

6. Breathing in, I see that the leaf
    functions non-locally.

    leaf, non-local

    Breathing out, I see how I function
    non-locally.

    I, non-local

7. Breathing in, I see that the leaf
    has accomplished its task from
    beginningless time.

    *leaf's task
    accomplished*

    Breathing out, I see that I have
    accomplished my task from beginning-
    less time.

    *my task
    accomplished*

8. Breathing in, I see that the leaf is
    already what it wants to become.

    *leaf is what it
    wants to be*

    Breathing out, I see that I am already
    what I want to become.

    *I am what I
    want to be.*

9. Breathing in, I see that the leaf can call   *leaf's past lives*
up all its lives from beginningless time.

Breathing out, I see that I too can call   *my past lives*
up all my past lives from beginningless
time.

This exercise is based on the insights of the Avatamsaka and Saddharmapundarīka Sutras. In the practice of mindfulness, the meditator can be in touch with the wonderful aspect of reality called the
Dharma realm (in Sanskrit, *dharmadhātu*). Here, they will discover
that neither they themself, nor anything that exists, is subject to
birth or death. The world that is limited by ideas and notions such as
the ideas of birth and death is called the ordinary world (in Sanskrit,
lokadhātu). In the Dharma realm, birth, death, being, and nonbeing
do not truly exist. Birth is only manifestation, and the same is true
of death. To be born is to manifest birth, and to die is to manifest
death. The appearance of a Buddha is not really the birth of a Buddha: it is just a manifestation, like that of an actor on a stage. The
leaf is the same. Although it seems to be born and to die, it does not
really do so. When it falls from the tree, it only appears to die, just
as a Buddha appears to pass away into nirvana. If a meditator can see
this, she will also see that her own birth and death are only a manifestation. In the Saddharmapundarīka Sutra (the Lotus Sutra), there
is a chapter on the life span of a Buddha, and one on the powers of a
Buddha. Someone who has learned to look at a Buddha in terms of
the Dharma realm can see the birthless and deathless nature of the
Buddha and realize that Buddha only appears to be born and to die.

The life span and the powers of a Buddha cannot be measured.
The life span of a leaf and the powers of a leaf are, like those of a
Buddha, immeasurable. The same can be said of each one of us.

The Saddharmapundarīka Sutra teaches us to distinguish three
dimensions: the historical dimension, the ultimate dimension, and

the dimension of action. The historical dimension is the phenomenological dimension in which we can say that the Buddha is born, is enlightened, teaches the Dharma, and passes away into nirvana. The ultimate dimension is the dimension where Buddha has been Buddha since beginningless time and has been teaching the Dharma and passing away into nirvana since beginningless time. The tower in which Buddha Prabhūtaratna sits—in the Saddharmapundarīka Sutra, we are told that this tower appears whenever and wherever the teachings of this sutra are given—refers to the ultimate dimension. Buddha Prabhūtaratna of the past can be touched in the present moment. Shakyamuni Buddha is indeed Prabhūtaratna Buddha. The dimension of action is that of the bodhisattvas, such as Samantabhadra, Avalokiteshvara, Bhaishajyaraja, Gadgadasvara, and Sadāparibhūta. All these bodhisattvas voyage in the historical dimension, teaching and helping all beings. Each has been a Buddha since times long past, and from the basis of the ultimate dimension, they open up the dimension of action. This means that they appear in the historical dimension, too, for that dimension is the framework for their actions.

If Buddha Shakyamuni and all other Buddhas have immeasurable life spans and powers, then the same is true of the leaf and of ourselves. The leaf has been a leaf for a long time already and is manifesting birth and death. We are the same.

The Saddharmapundarīka Sutra shows us that the Buddha is not an isolated appearance arising within the framework of space and time. The chapter called "Appearance of a Stupa" in the Saddharmapundarīka shows us that the Buddha has countless transformation bodies giving teachings in countless worlds simultaneously. The same is true of the leaf and of ourselves. Each of us has a transformation body in all places, and every action, thought, and word we speak has an influence on the ten directions. This exercise helps us enter a concentration. That concentration is called the saddharmapundarīka samādhi.

EXERCISE 10

Recognizing the Buddha in Me

1. Breathing in, I let the Buddha sit.   *Buddha sits*

    Breathing out, I do not need to sit.   *I do not need to sit*

2. Breathing in, I let the Buddha breathe.   *Buddha breathes*

    Breathing out, I do not need to breathe.   *I do not need to breathe*

3. Breathing in, the Buddha is sitting.   *Buddha is sitting*

    Breathing out, I enjoy the sitting.   *I enjoy the sitting*

4. Breathing in, the Buddha is breathing.   *Buddha is breathing*

    Breathing out, I enjoy the breathing.   *I enjoy the breathing*

5. Breathing in, the Buddha is the sitting.   *Buddha is the sitting*

    Breathing out, I am the sitting.   *I am the sitting*

6. Breathing in, the Buddha is the breathing.   *Buddha is the breathing*

    Breathing out, I am the breathing.   *I am the breathing*

7. Breathing in, there is only the sitting.   *only the sitting*

    Breathing out, there is no one sitting.   *no one sitting*

8.	Breathing in, there is only the breathing.	*only the breathing*
	Breathing out, there is no one breathing.	*no one breathing*
9.	Breathing in, there is peace while sitting.	*peace while sitting*
	Breathing out, there is joy while breathing.	*joy while breathing*
10.	Breathing in, peace is the sitting.	*peace is the sitting*
	Breathing out, joy is the breathing.	*joy is the breathing*

When we take refuge in the Buddha, we are taking refuge in a part of our own consciousness. Buddha is not someone's name. It is an epithet that means "awakened." All beings have this capacity to be awake and to realize understanding and compassion. The question is how to remain in touch with our Buddha nature and to keep it alive. This and the following exercises (11–15) help us to do this.

This meditation takes us from the historical to the ultimate dimension. At the beginning of the exercise, we see that the Buddha and the meditator are two separate entities. Have you ever felt lazy or at an impasse, and so not able to practice any more? At those moments, you can let the Buddha take over. It is just like when you, who are not a computer expert, are having problems with your computer. Suddenly a friend who is a computer expert turns up, and all you have to do for them to sort out your problem is let them sit down in your place.

The meditator, instead of struggling, allows their innate Buddha nature to take over. This exercise is based on the teaching that Buddha nature is not something acquired from without, but is always available in consciousness.

When we come to the sixth part of the exercise, we see that the agent is no longer separate from the action. The agent and the action have become one. It is like the sentence "The wind is blowing." We see that it is a tautology. If it is wind, it must be blowing. A wind that does not blow is not a wind at all. All we need is the word "wind." At this point, we touch the ultimate dimension where there is no separate self.

This exercise shows us that we can allow the Buddha nature to take over in any practice. As we brush our teeth or urinate, we can also witness that the Buddha is brushing our teeth or urinating.

Christian practitioners have enjoyed doing this exercise, since Buddha does not refer only to a historical personage but to an enlightened state of body and mind. A Christian practitioner can use the words "I let Jesus walk. I let Jesus breathe," since, according to Christianity, we are all children of God.

EXERCISE 11

Total Relaxation with the Buddha

1. Breathing in, Buddha is breathing gently.

    Buddha breathes

    Breathing out, I enjoy breathing gently.

    I enjoy breathing

2. Breathing in, the Buddha is lying down comfortably.

    Buddha is lying down

    Breathing out, I enjoy lying comfortably.

    I enjoy lying down

3. Breathing in, there is peace while breathing gently.

    peace while breathing

    Breathing out, there is joy while lying comfortably.

    joy while lying down

4. Breathing in, peace is the gentle breathing.

   peace is the breathing

   Breathing out, joy is the relaxation.

   joy is the relaxation

5. Breathing in, Buddha is breathing gently.

   Buddha is breathing

   Breathing out, Buddha is resting.

   Buddha is resting

6. Breathing in, I enjoy breathing gently.

   I enjoy breathing

   Breathing out, I enjoy resting.

   I enjoy resting

7. Breathing in, there is peace while breathing gently.

   peace while breathing

   Breathing out, there is joy while resting.

   joy while reasting

8. Breathing in, peace is the gentle breathing.

   peace is the breathing

   Breathing out, joy is the resting.

   joy is the resting

9. Breathing in, Buddha is breathing gently.

   Buddha is breathing gently

   Breathing out, I enjoy breathing gently.

   I enjoy breathing gently

10. Breathing in, Buddha is free.

    Buddha is free

    Breathing out, I enjoy the freedom.

    I enjoy being free

11. Breathing in, there is peace while breathing gently.

    peace while breathing

    Breathing out, there is joy while feeling free.

    joy while feeling free

12. Breathing in, peace is the gentle breathing.

    peace is the breathing

    Breathing out, joy is the freedom.

    joy is the freedom

This exercise is to help people relax in either the sitting or the lying position. The one who is guiding the exercise can repeat the phrases as many times as she feels is necessary to induce total relaxation. The important thing is to guide the practitioners in such a way that they do not need to make any mental effort and can relax completely. We can use it for ourselves when we are lying in bed to relax totally as we fall asleep.

EXERCISE 12

Touching the Buddha in Myself

1. Breathing in, the Buddha is breathing with my lungs.

   Buddha breathes with my lungs

   Breathing out, I enjoy the breathing.

   I enjoy my breathing

2. Breathing in, the Buddha is sitting with my back.

   Buddha sits with my back

   Breathing out, I enjoy the sitting.

   I enjoy the sitting

3. Breathing in, the Buddha dwells in   *Buddha dwells*
   the island of self.   *in island of self*

   Breathing out, I can dwell in the   *I dwell in island*
   island of myself.   *of myself*

4. Breathing in, the Buddha has arrived.   *Buddha has arrived*

   Breathing out, I enjoy arriving.   *I enjoy arriving*

This exercise, like the preceding ones in this chapter, is to help us be in touch with the Buddha nature in ourselves. It can be used anywhere, any time, even very briefly, when we need the support of the Buddha.

EXERCISE 13
I Have Arrived with the Buddha

---

1. Breathing in, I am aware: this is   *in-breath*
   the in-breath.

   Breathing out, I am aware: this is   *out-breath*
   the out-breath.

2. Breathing in, I follow my in-breath   *whole in-breath*
   from the beginning to the end.

   Breathing out, I follow the out-breath   *whole out-breath*
   from the beginning to the end.

3. Breathing in, I enjoy the in-breath.   *I enjoy the*
                                             in-breath

   Breathing out, I enjoy the out-breath.   *I enjoy the*
                                             out-breath

4. Breathing in, I am aware of my whole body.   *aware of body*

   Breathing out, I relax all my body.   *I relax my body*

5. Breathing in, I am aware: the Buddha has already arrived.   *Buddha has arrived*

   Breathing out, I am aware: the Buddha is no longer running. *no longer running*

6. Breathing in, I am aware: I have already arrived as the Buddha.   *arrived as the Buddha*

   Breathing out, I see I no longer need to run.   *no longer need to run*

7. Breathing in, I am aware: the Buddha dwells in the here.   *Buddha dwells in the here*

   Breathing out, I am aware: the Buddha dwells in the now.   *Buddha dwells in the now*

8. Breathing in, I am aware: I also dwell in the here.   *I dwell in the here*

   Breathing out, I am aware: I also dwell in the now.   *I dwell in the now*

9. Breathing in, I am aware of how solid the Buddha is.   *Buddha solid*

   Breathing out, I am aware of how free is the Buddha.   *Buddha free*

10. Breathing in, I feel solid.   *feeling solid*

    Breathing out, I feel free.   *feeling free*

11. Breathing in, Buddha enjoys
    interbeing.

    Breathing out, I enjoy interbeing.

*Buddha enjoys
interbeing*

I enjoy interbeing

EXERCISE 14
The Non-Self Nature of the Buddha and Myself

1. Breathing in, I see the Buddha seated
   before me.

   Breathing out, I bow before the
   Buddha with respect.

Buddha before me

I bow with respect

2. Breathing in, I see the Buddha in me.

   Breathing out, I see myself in the
   Buddha.

Buddha is in me

I am in the Buddha

3. Breathing in, I see the Buddha smile
   and the separation between me and
   the Buddha disappears.

   Breathing out, I smile and see no more
   separation between the one who bows
   and the one who is bowed to.

*Buddha and I not
separate*

*The one who bows
and the one who
is bowed to not
separate*

4. Breathing in, I see myself bowing
   deeply before the Buddha.

   Breathing out, I feel the Buddha's
   energy in me.

Bowing deeply

*Buddha's energy
in me*

This exercise is a continuation of the preceding one. It has also been practiced for more than a thousand years in the Buddhist tradition, when people prepare to touch the earth before the Buddha in ceremonies. After the incense offering and before touching the earth, the following words are usually recited: *The one who bows and the one who is bowed to are both by nature empty. Therefore the communication between them is inexpressibly perfect.* This reflection is based on the teachings of interdependent arising, emptiness, and non-duality. According to these teachings, the Buddha and the person who bows before him are interdependent and therefore empty of a separate self. Emptiness in Buddhism means the absence of a separate self. I am made of all that is not myself, including the Buddha. The Buddha is made of all that is not the Buddha, including myself. Thanks to this insight, a deep communication between myself and the Buddha is realized as I touch the earth. It is indeed unusual to see in religion such an equality between the one who worships and the one who is worshipped. Such a practice goes beyond all complexes of inferiority and superiority, and gives us confidence in our own awakened nature.

This exercise can be practiced in sitting meditation or as we bow deeply and touch the earth.

EXERCISE 15
The Infinity of Buddha and Myself

1. Breathing in, I see the Buddha before me.

   Breathing out, I see myself join my palms and bow in respect before the Buddha.

   Buddha before me

   join my palms
   in respect

2. Breathing in, I see the Buddha before me and behind me.

   Buddha before and behind me

   Breathing out, I see myself bow deeply to the Buddha before and behind me.

   bow deeply

3. Breathing in, I see Buddhas everywhere as many as the grains of sand in the Ganges.

   Buddhas everywhere

   Breathing out, I see myself everywhere as many grains of sand in the Ganges bowing to each one of them.

   Myself everywhere bowing to each Buddha

This exercise is a continuation of the preceding one. It has also been practiced for more than a thousand years in the Buddhist tradition. The original wording of the reflection before touching the earth has these words: *The practice center that I see before me is the jewelled net of Indra, made of countless precious jewels. All the Buddhas of the ten directions appear reflected in each of the precious jewels, and my own image standing before each of the Buddhas is also reflected in each of the precious jewels. As I bow my head before one Buddha, I am paying homage to all the Buddhas in the ten directions at one and the same time.*

The source of this meditation is the Avatamsaka Sutra. It is based on the principle that one is all and all is one. It helps us to see ourselves beyond the scope of the five aggregates, which are always limited by the framework of space and time. It also helps us to see how we interpenetrate every wonder of our universe.

This exercise, like the preceding one, can be practiced in the sitting position or as we bow deeply.

EXERCISE 16

Taking Refuge in the Island of Self

1. Breathing in, I come back to myself.   *coming back*

   Breathing out, I take refuge in my   *taking refuge in*
   own island.   *myself*

2. Breathing in, my mindfulness is   *mindfulness*
   the Buddha.   *is Buddha*

   Breathing out, my mindfulness   *shining near and far*
   shines near and far.

3. Breathing in, my conscious breathing   *breathing is*
   is the Dharma.   *Dharma*

   Breathing out, the conscious breathing   *guarding body*
   guards my body and mind.   *and mind*

4. Breathing in, my five skandhas are   *skandhas are*
   the sangha.   *sangha*

   Breathing out, my skandhas are   *practicing in*
   practicing in harmony.   *harmony*

We can practice this meditation anywhere and at any time, especially when we find ourselves in a state of anxiety and agitation and do not know what is best to do. It is an exercise in taking refuge in the Buddha, the Dharma, and the sangha. As we practice this meditation, it takes us directly to a place of peace and stability, to the most calm and stable place we can go. Buddha taught: "Be an island unto yourself. You should take refuge in yourself and not in anything else." This island is right mindfulness, the awakened nature, the foundation of stability and calm that resides in each of us. This island is also the Dharma, or the teachings of the Awakened Ones that show us the way and help us see what we need to do and what we should not do at any moment. Finally, this island is also the sangha body, or our practice community. When our five skandhas are in harmony with each other, we have peace. Our nervous and cardiovascular systems are soothed and calmed. Conscious breathing is what brings about this relaxation and peace. If we know that we are doing what is best in a difficult moment, we shall see that we no longer have any reason to be anxious or agitated. Is there anything better we could possibly do than that?

Say you were on an airplane, and the pilot announced that the plane was in trouble and might crash; this exercise would enable you to calm yourself and clear your mind. By bringing the Buddha, the Dharma, and the sangha back to your own island to show you the way and be a place of refuge for you, you would be able to feel safe. If you were indeed to die, you would be able to die beautifully, as you have lived beautifully, in mindfulness. You would have enough calm and clarity in that moment and would know exactly what to do and what not to do.

In the Sutra on Taking Refuge in Oneself,[1] the Buddha teaches his disciples to take refuge in their own island. The above exercise is based on that teaching. If you have memorized the song "Being an Island unto Myself," you can use it as a guided meditation as you sit.[2]

---

1. Samyuktagama 639, Samyutta Nikaya 47, 14.
2. For all songs, please refer to http://plumvillage.org/library/songs/.

EXERCISE 17

Touching Nirvana

1. Breathing in, I see the elements,   *earth, water, air*
   earth, water, and air in myself.   *in me*

   Breathing out, I smile to these   *I smile*
   elements in myself.

2. Breathing in, I see clouds, snow, rain,   *clouds, snow, rain,*
   rivers in myself.   *rivers in me*

   Breathing out, I see the atmosphere,   *atmosphere, wind,*
   wind, and forests in myself.   *forests in me*

3. Breathing in, I see mountains, oceans,   *Mother Earth in me*
   Mother Earth in me.

   Breathing out, I am with Mother   *most beautiful*
   Earth, the most beautiful planet in our   *planet in galaxy*
   galaxy.

4. Breathing in, I see the element light   *light in me*
   in me.

   Breathing out, I am made of light, of   *I am made of*
   sunshine.   *sunshine*

5. Breathing in, I see the sun as the un-   *my unfailing source*
   failing source of the food I consume   *of food*
   every day.

   Breathing out, like Buddha Shakya-   *I am a child of*
   muni, I am a child of Father Sun.   *of Father Sun*

6. Breathing in, I am the sun and   *smile to sun in me*
    I smile to the sun in myself.

    Breathing out, I am a star, one of   *I am a star*
    the largest in our galaxy.

7. Breathing in, I see the stars and the   *I am stars*
    galaxies in me.

    I am part of the immortality of stars   *immortality of stars*
    and galaxies.

8. Breathing in, I smile to the clouds   *smile to clouds*
    in my tea that never die.   *in tea*

    Breathing out, I am part of the   *immortality of*
    immortality of clouds.   *clouds*

9. Breathing in, I see all my ancestors   *the ancestors in me*
    in me, mineral, plant, animal, human,
    and spiritual.

    Breathing out, I see these ancestors   *their immortality*
    always alive in each of my cells and I
    am part of their immortality.

10. Breathing in, I see nothing is pro-   *nothing produced*
    duced, nothing destroyed, everything   *nothing destroyed*
    is transforming.

    Breathing out, I see the no birth and *no birth, no death of*
    no death of matter and energy.   *matter and energy*

11. Breathing in, I see that birth, death, *birth and death*
    being, non-being are only ideas.   *only ideas*

    Breathing out, I smile to my true   *smile to my nature*
    nature of no birth and no death.   *of no birth and no*
                                           death

12. Breathing in, free from birth and   *no more fear*
    death I have no more fear.

    Breathing out, I touch nirvana, my   *I touch nirvana*
    nature of no birth and no death.

EXERCISE 18

The Sixteen Exercises of the Sutta on the Full Awareness of Breathing[3]

1. Breathing in, I know this is the   *in-breath*
   in-breath.

   Breathing out, I know this is the   *out-breath*
   out-breath.

2. Breathing in, I follow the whole   *whole length of*
   length of the in-breath.   *in-breath*

   Breathing out, I follow the whole   *whole length of*
   length of the out-breath.   *out-breath*

3. Breathing in, I am aware of my   *aware of whole*
   whole body.   *body*

   Breathing out, I am aware of my
   whole body.

4. Breathing in, I calm my whole body.   *I calm my body*

   Breathing out, I release all the   *I release tensions*
   tensions in my body.

---

3. The complete sutta with commentary can be found in Thich Nhat Hanh, *Breathe! You Are Alive: Sutra on the Full Awareness of Breathing* (Berkeley, CA: Parallax Press, 1990).

5. Breathing in, I give rise to a feeling of joy.   *I give rise to joy*

   Breathing out, I feel joyful.   *I feel joyful*

6. Breathing in, I give rise to happiness.   *I give rise to happiness*

   Breathing out, I feel happy.   *I feel happy*

7. Breathing in, I am aware of my feelings.   *feelings*

   Breathing out, I am aware of an unpleasant feeling.   *unpleasant feeling*

8. Breathing in, I calm my feelings.   *I calm my feelings*

   Breathing out, I calm the unpleasant feeling.   *I calm the unpleasant feeling*

9. Breathing in, I am aware of a mental formation.   *mental formation*

   Breathing out, I calm the mental formation.   *calm*

10. Breathing in, I allow my mind to be peaceful and happy.   *my mind happy*

    Breathing out, I smile.   *I smile*

11. Breathing in, I concentrate my mind.   *concentrate mind*

    Breathing out, I am focused.   *focused*

12. Breathing in, I liberate my mind.   *liberate mind*

    Breathing out, I am free.   *free*

13. Breathing in, I contemplate the   *impermanence of all*
    impermanence of all things.

    Breathing out, I smile to the   *smile*
    impermanence of all things.

14. Breathing in, I contemplate the unde-   *undesirability of*
    sirability of what I crave.   *what I crave*

    Breathing out, I smile to the undesir-   *I smile*
    ability of what I crave.

15. Breathing in, I contemplate the   *no-birth, no-death*
    no-birth, no-death nature of all
    that is.

    Breathing out, I smile to the no-birth,   *I smile*
    no-death nature.

16. Breathing in, I contemplate letting go.   *letting go*

    Breathing out, I smile.   *smile*

EXERCISE 19

Mettā Meditation

May I be peaceful, happy, and light in body and spirit.

May I be safe and free from injury.

May I be free from anger, fear, and anxiety.

May I learn to look at myself with the eyes of understanding and love.

May I be able to recognize and touch the seeds of joy and happiness in myself.

May I learn to identify and see the sources of anger, craving, and delusion in myself.

May I know how to nourish the seeds of joy in myself every day.

May I live fresh, solid, and free.

May I be free from attachment and aversion, but not be indifferent.

May you be peaceful, happy, and light in body and spirit.

May you be safe and free from injury.

May you be free from anger, fear, and anxiety.

May you learn to look at yourself with the eyes of understanding and love.

May you be able to recognize and touch the seeds of joy and happiness in yourself.

May you learn to identify and see the sources of anger, craving, and delusion in yourself.

May you know how to nourish the seeds of joy in yourself every day.

May you be able to live fresh, solid, and free.

May you be free from attachment and aversion, but not be indifferent.

This guided meditation is on mettā. This is a Pali word meaning "loving-kindness."

The meditation helps us practice loving our self and others in a most wholesome way. The mettā meditation is very ancient. It was practiced by yogis in India before the time of Shakyamuni Buddha. He himself practiced and taught this meditation. Thich Nhat Hanh has worded it in a way that is suitable for practitioners of meditation in our own time.

It has always been taught that we should be able to love and take care of ourselves in order to be able to love and take care of others. So when you are beginning the practice of loving-kindness, you should always start by wishing for yourself what is good, beautiful, and true. It is important to feel a real emotion of love and compassion for yourself; to recognize that you, just like anyone else, need and deserve happiness, safety, security, freedom from anger, and so on.

The fifth-century Sinhalese patriarch Buddhaghosa, in his work *The Path of Purification,* used the example of lighting a fire. He said that we must start the fire with dry wood, and we can add the wet wood later. The dry wood is our selves. As we are in touch with ourselves all the time, we know how much we need security, freedom from attachment, anger, and so on. Once the fire is lit, we can throw on the wet wood of someone who makes us suffer, realizing that they need security and freedom from anger and fear, just as we do. Traditionally, the order of practice is first, one's self; second, someone you love; third, someone who is neutral; and fourth, someone who has harmed you or with whom you have a difficulty. Sometimes we do not feel worthy to receive our own love. Perhaps we have been taught that we must always put others first and that to care for ourselves is selfish. If you find it is too difficult to first generate love and compassion for yourself, you can start the practice by sending good wishes to someone who is easy for you to love (a grandparent, a dear friend, even an animal). Then, when you go on to practice for yourself, you may like to add the words, "Just as I wish for my beloved one to be peaceful, may I too."

Even if it takes some days of practice to love yourself, you should not try to send love to someone who has harmed you before you can feel love for yourself. So you may spend the whole meditation time sending love to yourself. There is nothing wrong with that.

Loving-kindness meditation should be concrete and should come from our hearts. It is not made from abstract words or wishes. Its purpose is truly to transform your way of looking at others and at yourself. If love meditation does not do that, it could just be wishful thinking. If your meditation is successful, it will not only change the way you look at others; it will also change the way they look at you.

CHAPTER 4

Prefaces to Guide Meditation

uring the three-month Rains Retreat in 2004, Thich Nhat Hanh offered prefaces to guide the retreatants in their meditation. After listening to the prefaces, the retreatants would meditate in silence on what they had heard for forty minutes or so. You can either read one of the prefaces for yourself before you begin a silent period of meditation, or if you are meditating in a group, someone can read a preface aloud for everyone else. If you are reading the preface for others, you can do so very slowly, so that each word can gently enter the consciousness of those who are listening, and so they do not need to make any effort to remember. During your silent meditation that follows the reading of the preface, whenever your mind wanders, you recognize this. Then you can smile and return to your contemplation of the preface you have heard.

There are two parts to meditation: stopping and looking deeply. Stopping means to calm your mind. In order to look deeply and contemplate a subject, your mind needs to be calm. Some of the prefaces are directed to stopping, and others to looking deeply. You can choose the preface that best suits your state of mind on that day.

1

Generating Joy and Happiness

Dear Buddha, you have taught us how to generate joy and happiness to nourish our body and mind. When I breathe in, I know that this is an in-breath. When I breathe out, I know that this is an out-breath. When I have been enjoying my in-breath and out-breath for a couple of minutes, I will see that my in-breath is deeper and my out-breath slower.

Breathing in, breathing out, deep, slow.

This deeper and slower quality of my breathing brings me peace and happiness. As I breathe in, my body and my mind feel calm. As I breathe out, I feel at ease in my body and mind. I am sitting very straight. Breathing in, I smile and relax all the tiny muscles in my face. I smile to myself and to all my ancestors. As I breathe out, I relax my body and mind completely. I let go of all my plans, my worries, and my fears. Nothing is more important than the peace and freedom that I feel.

As I breathe in, I am stably rooted in the present moment. As I breathe out, I feel that this is the most wonderful moment of my life, and I can prolong it for as long as I like.

In, out.
Deep, slow.
Calm, ease.
Smile, release.
Present moment, wonderful moment.

2

Relaxation and Healing

Dear Buddha, I am sitting very straight, with my back and my spine upright. My head is not bent backward or forward. On my lips is a smile, so that all the muscles of my face can relax. My arms are relaxed by my side, so that all the tension in the muscles of my arms can be released. I am practicing to be aware of my in-breath and out-breath. I am practicing to be aware of my body and to relax my body. Breathing in, I am aware that this is the in-breath, and the in-breath is something wonderful. It is the proof that I am alive. When I breathe out, I am aware that this is my out-breath, and I smile to life. I recognize my breath, and I allow my breath to become deeper and more peaceful. I recognize my body and relax my body. I know that there is tension in my body, and it is making healing difficult. I know that whenever I allow my body to relax, and my mind is not worrying or thinking about the past or the future, my body has a chance to produce the energy of healing. I want my body to have the chance to heal during the whole time of this sitting meditation.

Breathing in, I know this is my in-breath. I recognize my in-breath. Breathing out, I know this is my outbreath. I recognize my out-breath. I smile to it. I allow it to be peaceful. I know that this is my body as I breathe in, and I smile to my body as I breathe out. As I breathe out, I allow my body to be peaceful. Practicing like this, I feel at ease, peaceful, joyful, and I know that my body has a chance to heal.

3

Fully Present for Myself and All the Wonders of Life

Dear Buddha, it is still dark and I know that the cherry tree is out there in the courtyard in front of me. Soon the sun will rise. The birds will begin to sing. Butterflies will be fluttering and bees will be buzzing everywhere.

Dear Buddha, the cherry tree, the sun, and the birds are there for me, and I want to be there for them, full of freshness and beauty. I am surrounded by brothers and sisters, who are there for me as we sit in the meditation hall, and I want to be there for them with freshness and beauty.

Dear Buddha, I want to practice mindful breathing as you have taught us. When I breathe in, I am aware of that in-breath. I am fully present. What joy to be alive and to be breathing calmly and peacefully! I enjoy every moment of my in-breath. I become one with my in-breath. It is a source of peace and happiness for myself and for all my ancestors in me, because when I breathe in, all my ancestors in me breathe in. When I breathe out, I smile and enjoy my out-breath fully. I smile to the cherry tree, to the pine tree, to the sunrise, and to life in the present moment. I see how all my ancestors are smiling with me. How wonderful!

When I breathe, I completely relax all the muscles in my body. I let go of all tension. I do not struggle any more. I am completely relaxed. Breathing out, I smile to my whole body. Breathing in, my body and mind dwell in the present moment. I know that it is the only moment I can be alive and fully present. It is a wonderful moment. I am fully present for my sisters and brothers, for the cherry tree, the sunshine, the bees, and the butterflies.

4

Seeing Myself as a Flower, a Mountain, Still Water, Space

Dear Buddha, you are a flower, a wonderful flower, a rare flower, blooming in the garden of humanity. I am also a flower in the garden of humanity. I know I have to nourish my freshness for myself and for my sangha. Breathing in, I see myself as a flower in the garden of humanity. Breathing out, I feel fresh. Not only am I a flower; I can also be as solid as a mountain. When I have mindfulness, concentration, and solidity, I breathe in and see myself as a mountain. Breathing out, I feel solid. No words, no actions can make me lose myself. I cannot be swept away by thoughts about the past or the future. Breathing in, I see myself as a mountain. Breathing out, I feel solid. With mindfulness and concentration in me, my mind becomes peaceful, and my perceptions are not distorted or wrong. Breathing in, I see myself as still water. Breathing out, I reflect everything as it is.

Solid and free, I have as much freedom as the moon floating in the great vault of the sky; I am vast, peaceful. Breathing in, I feel a lot of space inside me and around me. Breathing out, I feel free.

5

Looking Deeply into Suffering to Develop Understanding and Compassion

Dear Buddha, we want to look deeply into our suffering and learn from it. Our suffering can be something that helps us grow in our spiritual life. By understanding our own suffering and the suffering of those around us, we discover the path we need to take. As an individual, a community, or a nation, we can always learn from our experience of suffering.

As a parent, an elder brother or sister, or a teacher, we generally have the tendency to use our authority to force our children, younger siblings, or students to do what we want. Doing this brings about suffering. We know that it is only by communication—using deep listening and being able to share—that we can transform the mountain of perceptions in ourselves and others. We know that whenever we use our authority as a parent, an elder sibling, or a teacher to force our children, younger siblings, or students to do something, we make them suffer, and we suffer ourselves.

China is one of the great powers that has forced other nations around it to submit to it, making those nations and itself suffer. Russia has learned the lesson of suffering from its invasion of Afghanistan, as has England. The United States has suffered from making war on Vietnam and Iraq. The Vietnam War brought about immense suffering, not only for the Vietnamese but also for the Americans. We pray that the US has learned from this suffering and will not inflict it again in other places.

Your teaching on the Four Noble Truths helps us open our eyes and leads us to learn from our suffering so that we do not repeat the mistakes we have made in the past. It gives us the capacity to contribute something to the awakening that will help our world have a greater opportunity in the future than it had in the past.

6

Opening My Heart

Dear Buddha, I know that your heart is a heart of compassion and love without any boundary, immeasurable and of great compassion. Your heart was able to embrace all species and all people. Dear Buddha, you frequently taught that when we open up our hearts in order to embrace all species and all people, we never suffer. You gave us the example that if we put a handful of salt into a bowl and stir it around, the water in the bowl will be so salty that it is undrinkable. But if we put a handful of salt into the river, we can all continue to drink the river water, which will not be undrinkable because of a handful of salt. Even if you put a whole box of salt into the river, the water would not be too salty to drink. The water in the bowl is very little, and the water in the river is immeasurable. The same is true of my heart. When I open my heart wide, the everyday things that normally make me displeased will not affect me. I shall be peaceful and joyful throughout the day because my heart has become wide and inclusive. Lord Buddha, I shall practice as you have taught, so that every day I can open my heart and include all my fellow practitioners and all people in it. I shall be able to see that those who do things that make me suffer do so because they themselves suffer a great deal, and my understanding will lead to love and acceptance.

7

Practicing Loving Speech Not Just with Words but Also with My Thoughts

Dear Buddha, even when I am silent, I continue to talk in my head. I talk not just with my mouth but also in my head, with my thoughts and my reflections. I vow to practice loving speech not just with the words of my mouth, but also in my thoughts.

I know that loving speech can bring me and those around me much happiness. I can produce this happiness simply by the way I speak. I know that compassionate speech is the most beautiful and noble kind of speech. I want to learn to speak in such a way that I can heal the wounds in myself and in other people.

Every time someone criticizes, judges, wounds, or makes me suffer, I am determined not to try to find ways to punish or take vengeance on the person. I shall simply come back to my breathing and then I shall look deeply to understand that person, to see that they suffer and do not know how to handle their suffering, and so pour it on to others. Thinking in this way, I can cultivate compassion in myself. Instead of punishing the other person, I embrace them in my loving thoughts. This practice heals my wounds and will heal the wounds in the other.

Dear Buddha, I know that I am very rich. I can offer much happiness by the gift of my words. I vow that from now on, I shall choose my words carefully, so that they reflect my love. When the other person receives that love, she will be healed, and I shall be healed as well. There is an art to choosing words.

8

Practicing Right Action to Manifest Compassion

Dear Buddha, the practice of Right Action is a way for our hearts to express compassion. Whatever I do needs to come from my heart of loving-kindness and compassion. The first training of

Right Action is the protection of life. I do my best never to destroy the lives of other living beings. That is a manifestation of a heart of compassion. The second training is generosity: offering my time and energy to help those who are suffering. I do not engage in bribery, corruption, or taking what is not given. The third training is protection from sexual misconduct. I protect children and others so that they do not become the victims of sexual misconduct. The fourth training is loving speech and deep listening, and the fifth is mindful consuming. These trainings are the way the Buddha has instructed me to practice Right Action, and I vow in my daily life to manifest my heart of compassion through these five trainings: not killing, not stealing, not committing sexual misconduct, engaging in loving speech and deep listening, and engaging in mindful consuming.

9

All I Can Take with Me Is the Fruit of My Actions

Dear Buddha, I know that I shall grow old, and old age is unavoidable. The day will come when I am sixty, seventy, or eighty years old. I will stoop, my legs will be weak, and my vision will be impaired. I know that sooner or later, I will fall sick. I shall be lying on my deathbed. There is no way I can escape that moment of lying on my deathbed. I shall take my last breath and, inexorably, I will die. At that time, I shall have to let go of everything: the people I love, the possessions I treasure, my land, my titles, diplomas, my position in society or the sangha. I shall have to abandon it all.

Dear Buddha, I know the only thing I shall take with me is the fruit of my actions. Everything I have thought, spoken, and done will follow me. Each one of my thoughts carries my signature. Each one of my words carries my signature. Each one of my actions carries my signature. I cannot say no to them. I cannot reject them. I cannot say they are not mine. So I must be careful when I give rise to a thought, some words, or an action, because I know that they are the only things I shall be able to take with me in the future.

10

Am I Tied by the Fetter of Attachment?

Dear Buddha, you are a free person. You were able to untie all the fetters that bound you, and you lived as a free person. You lived at ease. You have shown us what the fetters are, and you have called them by their names, so that we can see the ones we have not yet been able to untie. They are called the ten samyojanas, the ten internal knots, the ten internal formations. The first of them is attachment, expectations, yearnings. The second is ill-will, anger. The third is our wrong perceptions about ourselves and others. The fourth is our complexes, and the fifth is our suspicion and doubt. The sixth is thinking that this body is myself. The seventh is being caught in extreme views, pairs of opposites like being and non-being, birth and death, same and different. The eighth is the wrong views, the upside-down views, the perverse views. The ninth is being caught in our own ideas and perceptions and saying they are correct. The tenth is being caught in the outer form of rites and rituals.

Today, we are going to look deeply into the first fetter that is our attachment, to see if we are being tied by some yearning, by some expectation. As long as we have these yearnings, expectations, and desires, we are not free people. For instance, we may have a yearning to go live somewhere else. We have to be happy in the present moment. If we have happiness, then whether we are in another country or whether we are where we are now, we can be happy. Seeing old friends again can make us happy, but living with new friends can also make us happy.

We do not run after fame, authority, or power. There is no position in the sangha or the society that we yearn for. When we do not have these yearnings and attachments, or the need to attain something, we can be happy. If I see I still have a fetter of attachment and yearning that is binding me, I shall do my best to untie it so I can be free as you are, dear Buddha.

11

Untying the Third Fetter by Looking Deeply into What Is Nourishing It

Dear Buddha, you have shown us the first and second fetters, which are the fetters of attachment and hatred. Similarly, you have shown us the third fetter to be ignorance. We are aware that this fetter is the toughest and most persistent of all the fetters. It binds us and keeps us in the world of suffering, the world of birth and death.

Dear Buddha, you have taught that ignorance is the inability to see the way out of suffering, so we keep going around and around in a cycle of ill-being and birth and death. Your disciple Sariputra has shown us the way out of suffering and of birth and death. Ignorance is the inability to see our way. The teaching on the Four Noble Truths is the way out of suffering that the Buddha has shown us.

If we know how to recognize suffering and its roots far and near, we shall be able to see the path that leads us to peace, joy, and liberation. The path that leads to peace, joy, and liberation is the fourth Noble Truth, and to see the Four Noble Truths is to see our way. When we can do that, we no longer need to be afraid. We know that we are on the way out of suffering.

The Venerable Sariputra has taught us that we should observe our suffering in order to be able to see its cause in the way we are consuming. When we recognize the object of consumption that is making us suffer, we can stop consuming it, and automatically, we have the way out of our suffering. The items we consume can be edible, sense impressions, volitions, or consciousness.

We want to look deeply to see the nature of suffering and try not to run away from it anymore. We shall look courageously to identify its roots, in the way we consume with body and mind every day. There is edible food, sense-impression food, and volition food, which consists of my desires. Some of our most basic desires are keeping us in the prison of birth and death. Consciousness food is the collective consciousness that we participate in every day, and it can either take us on an unwholesome path or on the path of liberation. In our daily lives, we vow to look deeply so that our path can be lit up by the Four Noble Truths so we can untie the toughest of the ten fetters.

12

Untying the Fourth Fetter by Removing the Three Complexes of Superiority, Inferiority, and Equality

Dear Buddha, you have shown us the fourth fetter, which is complexes. Such complexes are the complex of superiority, the complex of inferiority, and the complex of equality. The reason why we are not free, why we suffer, why we are not able to be free, is because we have one of these three complexes. We know that all the complexes are based on our idea of a separate self. We think that there are separate selves, therefore we compare and think we are superior to, inferior to, or equal to others.

If we look deeply, we see that we and all species inter-are, that myself is because everything else is, and then we are not caught by an attachment to self. I see that my brothers and sisters are myself, and all that is beautiful and good in my brothers and sisters is also in me. My beauty and goodness is the beauty and goodness of my brothers and sisters. I do not think that a little bit of talent or a little bit of beauty can be a foundation for my personal happiness. It is freedom, the spirit of nondiscrimination, the spirit of non-self that bring real joy, peace, and liberation.

Dear Buddha, my brothers and sisters are a wonderful mani-

festation of life, and I am also a wonderful manifestation. If I look
at a chrysanthemum, I see that it is different from a lotus, and
a chrysanthemum does not need to be like a lotus in order to be
beautiful. Every phenomenon has its own beauty and goodness. I
see that I am also the chrysanthemum, and the chrysanthemum is
I. It is also the lotus. I know that only when I can remove the idea
of a separate self will I overcome the three complexes of superiority, inferiority, and equality.

13

Learning to Undo the Ninth Fetter: The Attachment to My Own Views

Dear Buddha, you have taught us that the ninth fetter is the fetter of being caught in my own view. It means that I hold tightly to
my opinion and feel that it is the absolute truth, which prevents
me from being able to accept any other truth as higher. I know
that most of us hold fast to our own opinions and feel they are the
supreme truth. In that way, we become narrow and lose the chance
for the truth to enter us and show us the way. I am determined to
look deeply in order to understand and let go of my own knowl-
edge and viewpoints so that I can hear those of others. Listening
deeply, I can discern the part that is correct and has right view.

As I touch the earth with my five limbs, I vow to let go of all
that I feel I have attained and all that I have understood so that the
nature of reality can manifest in me as the moon is reflected in the
waters of a clear lake.

14

I have arrived; I am home.

Father, I am sitting here with you. Mother, I am sitting here with
you. I am sitting with you, dear Teacher, dear sisters and brothers.
I have stopped running. I am not looking for anything anymore. I

have arrived. Peace and happiness are here and now. The Pure Land and the kingdom of God is in the present moment. I do not need to look for it. I breathe in, I am home. I breathe out, I have arrived. I have stopped. No more running.

15

Mother and Father, we have arrived; we are home.

Mother, I know you are in me, in every cell of my body. Father, I know you are in me, in every cell of my body. I am your continuation, just like the maize plant is the continuation of the seed of corn. Each time I breathe in, you breathe with me. Each time I smile, you smile, too.

Mother, throughout your whole life, you have worked hard, taking care of Father, of me, of my brothers and sisters, of your family, of Father's family. Rarely did you have the chance to sit calmly, to relax, to be free. Now, I am sitting for you, and you are sitting with me. We have time, and there is no need for us to worry about anything.

Mother, Father, let's release all the tensions in our body and mind. Let us be at home, let us arrive. Let us breathe together. Let us be free and smile together right now in the present moment. My joy and happiness are your joy and happiness. We are sitting together. We are dwelling in the present moment, free, peaceful, and happy.

16

Dear ancestors, we have arrived; we are home.

I breathe in, and I feel I have arrived. I breathe out, I feel I am at home. Dear Buddha, I have arrived in the here and now. It is my true home. I feel fully alive. I have arrived, and therefore I can touch the wonders of life. In the present moment, the Pure Land, the kingdom of God, are available right now.

I have always been running in my past lives, and I am still running in this life. I do not want to run anymore; I want to stop. I want to arrive in my true home, in each moment. I want to come home to myself. When I breathe in, I am free. I am in the kingdom of God, in the Pure Land of Buddha. When I breathe out, I smile. Every breath helps me to arrive, to come home, to dwell in the present moment, to be free and at peace, able to touch deeply the wonders of life.

Dear Buddha, I know that each time I succeed in coming home to myself, freedom, joy, and happiness become possible. The same is true for my parents and for my ancestors in me; they can also all come home. This can happen in the space of just one in-breath or one out-breath. When I have truly arrived, I am free; there is nothing more to do. I can fully enjoy the Pure Land of Buddha, the kingdom of God, and all my ancestors in me can also enjoy, along with me.

17

I have arrived with my father, mother, and teacher.

Dear Buddha, as I breathe in, I see the presence of my father in myself. I don't see just a number of images of my father, but the reality of my father. My father's reality has been transmitted in its entirety to my reality. My father in me is sitting with me. I am holding my father's hand. Since I have been able to stop running, my father has also stopped running. We are both truly there for each other.

Dear Buddha, as I breathe in, I see my mother in myself. My mother is not a number of images that I have stored up. My mother is a reality. I am the continuation of my mother, and therefore I see that my mother in me is sitting with me. I am holding my mother's hand. My mother and I are there for each other. Thanks to my being able to stop running, my mother has also stopped running. My mother and I are dwelling peacefully in the present moment.

I also see my teacher in myself. I am sitting with my teacher. Because I have stopped running, I can see clearly the presence of my teacher, and my teacher and I can sit together whenever I want.

18

Aware of my breathing, I nourish myself and I nourish all my ancestors and descendants.

Dear Buddha, each time I contemplate a leaf, I see the leaf breathing. The leaf uses sunlight and carbon dioxide to create sap so that it can nourish itself and nourish the whole tree.

I do the same, dear Buddha. Each time I breathe, I nourish myself, not only with oxygen but also with mindfulness, concentration, insight, stability, and freedom. I nourish my parents in me and outside of me. I nourish my blood and spiritual ancestors in me and around me. I also nourish my brothers, my sisters, my children, my grandchildren, who are in me and around me. I am breathing for all of them. I am the continuation of my parents, of all my ancestors. I am already continued by my brothers, my sisters, and my children in me and around me.

Dear Buddha, each time I breathe, I also nourish the Buddha in me.

19

I am a river, a continuation of my blood and spiritual ancestors.

Dear Buddha, looking deeply into my physical body, I can see the four elements: earth, water, air, and fire. I see them working together inside my own body and interacting with the four elements outside. If I am the four elements within my body, I am also the four elements without. Thanks to this interaction and interpenetration, I do not identify myself as this body, made up of organs such as the heart, the lungs, the liver, the kidneys . . . Without the four elements, these organs could not exist. I can calmly declare that my body is the four elements and the four elements are my body.

But my body is not only these four elements. The four elements and my body are neither the same nor different. It is the same for myself. I cannot manifest without this body and its organs. I know that I am not only this body and these organs; however, I could not be me without them, either.

The four elements are continually changing, so my body too is always changing. My body is a river, and I too am a river. I see that I am the continuation of my blood and spiritual ancestors. Looking into myself, I can see all of them. When I am able to generate the energy of compassion and insight to bring understanding, in that instant, I bring understanding to all my ancestors and descendants.

20

I am the Buddha's continuation.

Dear Buddha, you have helped to bring alive my spiritual life. You are not sitting on the altar; you are present in every cell of my body. You are my teacher and I am your continuation. Each time I breathe in, I am aware of the miracle of life in me and around me. Each time I make a step, I can touch the wonders of the Pure Land and the kingdom of God in me and around me. You and I are not two separate entities. I make the vow to be your beautiful continuation, so that I can help all beings to wake up, all those who live in confusion and forgetfulness. Dear Buddha, I am sitting for you and you are sitting for me.

21

Being a Buddha in the Here and Now

Dear Buddha, breathing in, I can see you sitting up straight in the lotus position in every cell of my body. I am sitting with your back, very straight yet supple. My shoulders have let go of all tension, and I offer a half-smile. All the muscles in my body are relaxed. You breathe in and you breathe out, dear Buddha. In this moment, you do not need to go anywhere, and you have nothing to do. I know that you and I are not two separate entities. I can see you sitting as a free person. I see you enjoying breathing in deeply and touching all the wonders of life in you and around you. I see you breathing out and smiling. I know that it is possible for me to become a buddha right now in this present moment, completely free from the past and the future.

22

I am clouds; I am snow.

Dear Buddha, I see that I am the ocean; all the rivers on the planet earth are pouring into me.

I see myself as vapor turning into a cloud, enjoying my time traveling across the sky and turning into rain, snow, or hail that falls on the peaks of mountains and immense forests.

I see myself turning into streams of water, which gradually return to the ocean. I bring life to millions of people, millions of species, to the trees, the earth, refreshing them, nourishing and healing life. I know I am on my way back to the ocean, but I am not in a hurry, because right now I have become the ocean; I already am the ocean.

I am this particular river, but I am also other rivers. There has never been a time when I have not been water, I have not been the ocean. That is why I am not in a hurry. I just enjoy my time moving along, using my time to make life and all species beautiful.

Dear Buddha, you are also the ocean. You have also been clouds, snow, and rivers. You continue to be the ocean, clouds, snow, and rivers. You are not just one river. You are many rivers, and I am the same. You have brought so much beauty, joy, and relief to living beings. I am in you and you are in me. We share the nature of all manifestations.

23

My thoughts are led by the insight into impermanence and non-self.

Dear Buddha, I know that the first noble truth is suffering and the third noble truth is happiness. Just as suffering can be superficial or deep, there are happinesses that are on the surface and happinesses that are deep. We know that the fourth noble truth is the path that leads to happiness and puts an end to suffering.

The fourth noble truth is the Noble Eightfold Path, which begins with Right View, the view that is in accord with reality. The view that accords with reality is, according to the Buddha, the insight into impermanence and no-self. When I have that insight, my thinking, speech, and actions will not bring about suffering. Instead, they will bring about happiness. Whatever I learn about the Dharma, then contemplate and put into practice, will contribute to bringing my thinking, speaking, and acting into accord with right view. When I am determined to learn, contemplate, and apply the practice, my actions of body, speech, and mind will be in accord with right view.

I want to practice in such a way that in every moment of my daily life, as I look and observe phenomena, I shall see their nature of impermanence and no-self. That is the basic practice taught by the Buddha. I see that my body and my mind are impermanent and the world is impermanent. I see that I am not a separate self, but a drop of water in a river, a cell in a body, always in a state of change.

Seeing this nature of no-self and impermanence, I have right view as the compass for all that I think. When my thoughts are guided by right view, right thinking will occur.

24

Everything is impermanent and without a separate self, and everything is a continuation.

Dear Buddha, I am practicing to do as Bodhisattva Avalokiteshvara did, looking deeply into the five aggregates that make up my body and mind as rivers: the rivers of body, feelings, perceptions, mental formations, and consciousness. I can see how my body is impermanent, being born and dying at every moment, as are my feelings, perceptions, mental formations, and consciousness.

I can see that there is continuation, but this continuation is based on birth and death taking place at every moment. I do not want to be deceived by this form of continuation, because I can see that that there is nothing that can survive unchanged forever. At each moment, phenomena are born and die, and at the same time, there is continuation. This kind of continuation does not mean that there is an entity that is permanent and eternal. It is what the Buddha called *no-self.*

I am practicing to see the impermanent and no-self nature of the five aggregates. Even when I am not practicing sitting meditation, I vow to keep looking and listening with the insight that everything is born and dies. Nothing is permanent, but there is continuation, though that continuation is not a separate self.

25

Sitting with the Awareness of All Beings of the Past, Present, and Future

Dear Buddha, in the place where I am sitting now, it may have been that tens of millions of years ago, an enlightened one arose who shone light for the world. In the place where I am sitting, millions of beings have been born, and millions of beings have died.

As I sit in this place in the present moment, I am aware that I am truly present in this place and in this moment. My mind is able to embrace all of time, past, present, and future. My mind is able to embrace the whole of the trichiliocosm. I know that all of us are sitting here, and I am truly present.

I am sitting for all the people and all the beings that have been born and that have died here. I am sitting for the people who will be born in the very place I am sitting for millions of years to come, and for the people who will lie down here to die for millions of years to come.

I wish that in five hundred million years to come, people will sit as I am sitting and be aware that five hundred million years previously, someone practiced sitting meditation here, and with their mind, embraced all of time and space and sat as an enlightened one. I am breathing mindfully with this awareness, and I am embracing endless time and infinite space in clear awareness.

26

Like chrysanthemum flowers in a pot, we all come from the same roots.

Dear Buddha, it is autumn, and we have pots of chrysanthemums in our meditation center. As we contemplate the pots of chrysanthemums, it seems they are giving us a Dharma talk about no-self, interbeing, and non-duality. Some of the plants just have seven or ten branches, and each branch bears one large flower. They are of the large-headed variety. There are pots that bear as many as one hundred flowers. Some of them are still buds, some are opening, and some are fully bloomed. If the flowers were to look down at their root system, they would see that they all came from the same source and the same root.

All of us belong to the same sangha. We resemble a pot of chrysanthemums that has one hundred flowers. Every flower has its own beauty and fragrance. Each one of us has a little mindfulness and a little compassion, and we all belong to the same sangha and share the same root system. If we look deeply, we see that each one of us is not just one flower or one branch but a whole pot of flowers. I am this particular chrysanthemum flower, but I am also the other flowers, because we are all one sangha and we share our roots. There are excellent roots and there are roots that have one or two difficulties, but we are practicing to transform them. Each one of us can see that we are a flower, but we are also able to see that we are the roots and the whole pot of flowers. I am also my elder brother or sister. I am also my younger brother or sister. I am also my teacher and my ancestral teachers. Whatever happens to me, happens to the whole sangha. Whatever happens to one member of the sangha, happens to me and to the whole sangha. I see clearly the interbeing, no-self, and non-dual nature of the chrysanthemum flower and of every member of the sangha. With this insight, I am able to live peacefully, joyfully, harmoniously, and happily.

27

I am the universe, limitless time and infinite space.

Dear Buddha, when I look deeply into my body and mind, I see the four elements: earth, water, fire, air. I see the four elements within me and outside of me are in a constant state of interchange. I see hundreds of thousands of beings in me: all the animal and plant species, as well as the earth, minerals, rocks, and dust of the stars.

I see my human ancestors, my animal ancestors, my plant and mineral ancestors in me. I also see my descendants and future generations in me, preparing to manifest in the future.

I see my body and mind as an uninterrupted stream that has no beginning and will have no end. This stream is in a constant state of change, flowing onward like a river without ever stopping. In it, there is nothing changeless, nothing eternal. Thoughts, feelings, and mental formations keep replacing each other in order to manifest. There is no core and no self. I see how I am my ancestors and I am my descendants. I see that I appear in the form of the universe, stars, galaxies, mountains, rivers, vegetation, trees, and animals. I also carry within myself infinite time and endless space.

28

All phenomena are in a state of transformation and continuation, without a separate self.

Dear Buddha, every time I step on a golden autumn leaf, I am in touch with the no-birth, no-death nature of the leaf. I know that the leaf has not died. It is just in a state of change on its way to becoming something else. A leaf can be continued by new forms of life, including a new leaf. For the whole of its life on the tree, it works to nourish the tree and to nourish itself. When it falls from the tree, it can see that it is in the tree and it is in the other leaves. So the leaf falls from the tree very beautifully, selflessly, and fearlessly.

I know that birth and death are happening in every moment. Birth and death happen without there having to be a separate self. If there were a separate self, it could not be born or die. That is why we are practicing to be able to see that through all the changes and transformations that take place, there is a continuation that does not need a changeless, permanent subject.

29

Practicing Like a Leaf to Nourish Myself and My Sangha

Dear Buddha, every time I look at a leaf, I learn so much from it. Each leaf spends its whole life producing nutriments to nourish itself and nourish other leaves, as well as nourishing the whole tree. All the leaf wants to do is to protect, support, and nourish, and never has a wish to punish, blame, or envy.

As a member of the sangha, I wish to practice to be like a leaf. Every day, I vow to generate joy, happiness, compassion, and loving-kindness to nourish myself and to nourish the other members of the sangha. I want to help the sangha to grow more beautiful and stronger every day. I vow not to blame, envy, criticize, or disparage but to use the compassion and loving-kindness I have generated to support, uphold, shine light on, and help other members of the sangha. I know that if I can be as a leaf, I shall be happy and help the sangha to be more beautiful and happier every day.

30

Taking Refuge in the Sangha in Order to Be Free

Dear Buddha, how lucky we are to have a sangha to take refuge in. The Sangha Jewel is one of three precious jewels, and in the sangha we can flow as a river, the river of the sangha.

When I take refuge in the sangha, I feel solid. I know my way ahead. I entrust my difficulties, suffering, and expectations to the sangha body so that the sangha can carry me along on a path to the future.

In the world, there are many people who lead very lonely lives. They do not have a place of refuge and do not know the direction in which they are going. They do not know what the purpose of their life is. I am very lucky to have the sangha to take refuge in.

In the sangha, everyone is doing their best to practice. Thanks to that, in the sangha body we can find the Buddha body and the Dharma body.

Taking refuge in the Three Jewels brings each of us much happiness. We vow to entrust our lives to the sangha, to commend all our yearnings and wishes to the sangha. We want to commit our difficulties and suffering to the sangha so that the sangha can embrace us. We shall be able to take every step in freedom on the path of our ideal, like a river that knows the way downstream to the ocean.

Sitting here with the sangha, breathing in rhythm with the sangha, and receiving the energy of the sangha, I feel safe and happy.

CHAPTER 5

Touching the Earth

*T*rees have roots; water has its source. As human beings, we also have our roots and our source. They are our ancestors, our family, our culture, our country of birth or adoption; all that is most familiar and dear to us. A tree is at its most beautiful and flourishes when it is well-supported and nourished by many strong roots. We are the same. We are happy and healthy when we feel supported and nourished by our ancestors, our family, our country. On the other hand, if we are feeling alienated and disconnected from our roots, we feel lost, lonely, and we suffer. If we suffer, it is not because we do not have roots; in fact, they are always there. But maybe we have deliberately cut ourselves off from them or rejected them?

The practice of Touching the Earth is a meditation that helps us to return to the earth, to rediscover our roots, and to recognize all the beauty that we have not been able to see until now. As soon as we can accept our roots, their weaknesses along with their strengths, we will feel reconnected to a stream of spiritual and genetic ancestors. We do not need to go far to discover our ancestors. They are still alive in us. It is enough to practice touching the earth to get in contact with them, to feel their energy circulating in us. This practice reminds us that we too are the earth, and we are a part of life. We are no longer lonely, lost children without a refuge. On the contrary, we feel grounded and solid. Suffering will be replaced by peace and happiness.

The position of our body touching the earth helps our meditation. It can be compared with certain poses in hatha yoga that help us become calm and focus our minds. To practice the touching-the-earth position, first, stand up straight with palms joined, making a lotus bud. Bring your joined palms up to the level of your forehead and touch your forehead with your two thumbs. Say quietly to yourself, *"With my brain."* Now bring your joined palms down to the level of your heart and say quietly to yourself, *"With my heart."* Spread your arms out at both sides of your body and contemplate, *"With my whole body."* Now bend forward, moving toward the ground. Before your knees reach the ground, place your hands on the floor, on either side of the place where you will lay your forehead. When kneeling, your forehead touches the ground, the back of your thighs resting on the back of your calves; your whole body is close to the earth. Your forearms are in contact with the earth on either side of your forehead, your palms facing upwards. The significance of the upturned palms is that you have nothing to hide, and you open your heart wide to receive insight as you touch the earth.

If, because of physical limitations, these two positions are not possible, you can sit on a chair, leaning forward toward the earth, or simply join your palms and bow your head.

In whatever position you have chosen, with your four limbs and forehead touching the earth, completely relax your body and mind so that you can visualize and look deeply into the images evoked by the text as it is being read.

Breathe in the strength and stability of the earth, and as you breathe out, release all your suffering. If you wish, you can first spread a clean cloth on the ground. During the practice, your face will be in close contact with the ground for some time, and with a cloth, you can avoid breathing the dust.

This practice can transform your situation and will help toward building your sangha. After three months of practice, you will see real changes in your relationships with yourself and with those around you.

FIRST EXERCISE

The Five Earth Touchings

(Before touching the earth, the practitioner first reads the words below in italics, either aloud or silently. Whilst prostrating, the practitioner contemplates the text that follows. If practicing in a group, one person can read the text aloud while the others touch the earth and contemplate.)

FIRST EARTH TOUCHING

Touching the earth, I connect with all generations of my blood ancestors.

(With the sound of the bell, the practitioner or the whole group touches the earth.)

I see you, Father, Mother. Your blood, your flesh, and your vitality are circulating in my veins, nourishing every cell. Through you, I see each of my grandparents. Your energy, your expectations, your experience, and your wisdom have been transmitted to me from so many generations. I carry in me the life, blood, happiness, and sorrow of all my ancestors. Suffering and shortcomings have also been passed on to me, and I am practicing to transform them. I open my heart, my flesh, my bones to receive the energy of your insight and love, as well as of your experience. I see my roots in you, Father, Mother, grandfathers, grandmothers. I know that I am just your continuation. Please support, protect, and transmit to me still more of your energy. I am aware, dear ancestors, that wherever your children or grandchildren are living, you are present. I know that you always love and support your children and grandchildren, even though you were not always able to express your love skillfully due to your own difficulties and challenges. Dear ancestors, I am aware that you have done your best to build a way of life based on gratitude, loyalty, confidence, respect, and love. As a continuation of your lineage, I touch the earth with all my heart and allow your energy to penetrate me. I turn to you, my blood ancestors, to ask for your support, protection, and strength.

(Three breaths, then with the sound of the bell, the practitioner or the whole group stands up.)

SECOND EARTH TOUCHING

Touching the earth, I connect with all generations of my spiritual ancestors.

(With the sound of the bell, the practitioner or the whole group touches the earth.)

I see you in me, my spiritual teachers, who guide me on the path of love and understanding, who have taught me to breathe mindfully, to smile, to forgive, to live deeply in the present moment. Through you, I can be in touch with many generations and traditions of spiritual teachers, saints, and spiritual ancestors,[1] going back to the ones who began my spiritual tradition thousands of years ago. Your energy enters me and creates peace, joy, understanding, and love in me to this day. I know that your energy has deeply transformed the world. Without you, I would not know the way of practice that brings peace and happiness into my life and into the life of my family and society. I open my heart, my body, and my mind to receive your experience, your wisdom, and your energy of love and protection. I am your continuation. I ask you, dear spiritual ancestors, to transmit to me your infinite source of energy, peace, stability, understanding, and love. I make the vow to practice in order to transform my suffering and the suffering of the world and to transmit your energy to future generations.

(Three breaths, then with the sound of the bell, the practitioner or the whole group stands up.)

1. Here, you can add the names of spiritual ancestors appropriate for the practitioners present.

THIRD EARTH TOUCHING

Touching the earth, I connect with this land and all the land ancestors who have made it available to us.

(With the sound of the bell, the practitioner or the whole group touches the earth.)

I see that I am whole, protected, and nourished by this land and by you, who have made life easy and possible for me here by all your efforts. I am filled with gratitude toward all the generations of you who have lived on, worked, and developed this land. I am aware that thanks to you I have all I need.

I see *(here you should insert the names of those who have helped build the country in which you are practicing)* . . . you who have used your talents, your wisdom, your patience to make this country a refuge for many people coming from all over the world. Whether your names are remembered or not, you have built schools, hospitals, cathedrals, roads, bridges, etc. Wholeheartedly, you have worked for human rights and justice, building brotherhood and sisterhood. You have advanced our understanding of the world through your curiosity and scientific research and made our lives easier. I feel your harmonious presence when walking in nature, you who have lived in peace on this land and who have known how to protect the Earth. Today, I also wish to live in harmony with all species, and I feel the energy of this land penetrate my body and spirit, accepting me and supporting me. I make the vow to continue to cultivate this energy and to transmit it to future generations. I am determined to practice for the transformation of violence, hate, discrimination, and ignorance, which still exist in society, so that future generations will know joy and peace. May you and this land give me protection and support.

(Three breaths, then with the sound of the bell, the practitioner or the whole group stands up.)

FOURTH EARTH TOUCHING

Touching the earth, all the energy I have received from
all my ancestors I transmit to those I love.

(With the sound of the bell, the practitioner or the whole group
touches the earth.)

The unlimited energy I have received, I now transfer to you, Father, Mother, and everyone I love. In the past, you have suffered and worried because of me and for my sake. I know I have been unskillful and foolish due to not being mindful enough in my daily life. I know that you who love me have also suffered from your own difficulties. You have not always been lucky enough to have an environment that enabled you to flourish.

I transmit this wonderful source of energy to you, my mother, my father, my brother *(name)*, my sister *(name)*, my beloved *(name)*, my child *(name)*, to ease your pain and transform your suffering so that you will be able to smile again and feel the joy of being alive. With my whole heart, I wish for your physical and mental well-being, that you may be at peace and happy. Your happiness is my happiness. I promise to love and care for you, and I ask all my blood and spiritual ancestors to support and protect you. I see that I am not separate from you. I am one with those I love.

(Three breaths, then with the sound of the bell, the practitioner
or the whole group stands up.)

FIFTH EARTH TOUCHING

Touching the earth with understanding and compassion, I transmit to the one who has made me suffer the positive energy I have received from my ancestors.

(With the sound of the bell, the practitioner or the whole group touches the earth.)

I open my heart so that I can transmit to you the energy of understanding and love, you who have made me suffer or hurt me deeply. I know that you have also been through much suffering. Your heart may be overloaded with bitterness and anger. Because you have suffered, you make others suffer. I know that you have not been lucky. As a child or adolescent, you did not receive the love and care that you needed. Life and society have dealt you many hardships. You may have been wronged and abused. You have not been guided on the path of mindful living. You have accumulated many wrong perceptions about life and about me. As a result, you have made me and my dear ones suffer. I pray to my blood and spiritual ancestors to channel to you the energy of love and protection, so that your heart can receive the nectar of compassion and blossom like a flower. All I wish for is your transformation, that you can touch the joy of being alive, that you no longer hold on to the anger, resentment, and suffering in your heart and do not continue to make yourself and others suffer. I see that your suffering has been passed down from generation to generation. I do not want to hold feelings of anger and hatred toward you. I want your suffering to end. As my heart blossoms like a flower, I can let go of blame and resentment. I channel to you my energy of compassion and understanding, and I ask my ancestors to support you.

(Three breaths, then with the sound of the bell, the practitioner or the whole group stands up.)

SIXTH EARTH TOUCHING (OPTIONAL)

Touching the earth, I connect with my original spiritual tradition.

(With the sound of the bell, the practitioner or the whole group touches the earth.)

I see myself as a child, in the church, the mosque, the temple, or the synagogue, listening to a sermon or attending a ceremony. I see the priest, the imam, the rabbi, or other people from my congregation. A time may have come when I lost faith in the religion of my childhood. I was not able to communicate my difficulties and no one was able to resolve them. I abandoned my childhood faith and lost contact with the spiritual ancestors of that tradition. Having looked deeply, I am aware that there are treasures within the spiritual tradition into which I was born. This tradition has contributed to the stability, joy, and inner peace of my ancestors for generations. I know I can go back to it to rediscover its essential spiritual values, which can nourish myself and my children. As I touch the earth, I reconnect with my spiritual ancestors of my former faith and allow their energy to flow freely through me. I recognize all the teachers throughout the centuries in my former faith as my spiritual ancestors. I bow before you in the present moment, the only moment that truly counts.

(Three breaths, then with the sound of the bell, the practitioner or the whole group stands up.)

EXPLANATION

The Five Earth Touchings are above all a practice of reconciliation. After practicing the first two Earth Touchings, we feel the energy from our blood and spiritual families circulating in our body and mind. We already feel stronger and more confident.

During the third Earth Touching, we get in contact with our homeland, the sacred energy of nature, and the people who worked the land and built a nation. Many of them worked silently without leaving their names. Even though long dead, they are still present, protecting and supporting us. After this Earth Touching, we feel like a tree with many solid roots. We have more energy.

The fourth Earth Touching is directed toward our beloved ones with whom we share the sources of energy that we have just received. At the sound of the bell, when we stand up, the discrimination that we felt between ourselves and the other disappears. We and our beloved ones become one stream of life. Our peace and our happiness become theirs. If we have a lot of solidity and energy, we can transmit it to them.

During the fifth Earth Touching, we transmit our energy to those who have made us suffer. Practicing this Earth Touching for the first time, some people feel a lot of resistance. Why should we love and transmit our energy to that person who has hurt us and created so much difficulty? But regularly practicing this Earth Touching for several weeks, we come to understand how beneficial it can be.

Practicing wholeheartedly, after several months we will feel the hatred in our hearts dissolve. It is miraculous. Some practitioners have let us know that after only six months practice, they no longer felt the need to continue with this Earth Touching. None of the hatred remained toward the person who had made them suffer.

This is the authentic practice of compassion. The Buddha taught: do not answer hate with hate; the only response to hate is love and forgiveness. As long as we hold on to our hatred, we will continue to suffer. When we can put this teaching into practice, compassion fills our hearts. When we can forgive the other, we are healed. We will feel more at peace and at ease, touching well-being and happiness.

If we have suffered a lot and our wounds are very deep, we should practice the fifth Earth Touching every evening. To succeed, we must first succeed with the first two Earth Touchings. We need to get sufficiently in contact with our blood and spiritual ancestors to be able to receive their energy of love. At Plum Village, we practice

Touching the Earth together or individually in the meditation hall. Once we have become familiar with this practice and mastered it, we can adapt the text so that it is more appropriate to our own situation.

If you were brought up in a tradition other than Buddhism, a tradition that you have now abandoned, the sixth Earth Touching can help you return to and reconcile with your roots. To be in connection with your spiritual roots is very important for your solidity and healing. With two spiritual families ("double belonging"), you will be able to enrich your spiritual life with treasures from both roots, bringing you even more joy and love.

SECOND EXERCISE

The Three Earth Touchings

(Before touching the earth, the practitioner reads the words in italics below, either aloud or silently. While prostrating, the practitioner contemplates the text that follows. If practicing in a group, one person can read the text aloud while the others touch the earth and contemplate.)

FIRST EARTH TOUCHING

Touching the earth, I connect with my ancestors and descendants, from both my spiritual and blood families.

(With the sound of the bell, the practitioner or the whole group touches the earth.)

My spiritual ancestors are noble teachers, saints, martyrs, patriarchs, and matriarchs throughout the ages, and also my teachers of this lifetime. Whether you are still living or you lived long ago, you are all truly present in me. You have transmitted to me the seeds of peace, wisdom, love, and happiness. You have woken up in me seeds of peace, insight, compassion, and happiness.

When I look at you, my spiritual ancestors, I see those who are perfect in the practice of the mindfulness trainings, understanding, and compassion, and those who are still imperfect. I bow down and accept you all as my spiritual ancestors, knowing that within myself are shortcomings and weaknesses.

(three breaths)

Aware that my practice of the mindfulness trainings is not always perfect, and that I am not always as understanding and compassionate as I would like to be, I open my heart to my spiritual descendants and accept you all. Some of you practice the mindfulness trainings, understanding, and compassion in a way that invites confidence and respect. There are also those of you who are struggling with many difficulties and are constantly going through ups and downs in your practice. Aware of my own weaknesses and faults, I open my heart and accept you all.

(three breaths)

In the same way, I accept all of you, my ancestors, on my father's side and my mother's side of the family, with all your good qualities, your talents, and your virtuous actions, as well as your faults and your weaknesses.

(three breaths)

You, my spiritual and blood ancestors and descendants, are all present in me. I am you and you are me. I do not have a separate self. We are all part of a wonderful stream of life constantly flowing together.

(Three breaths, then with the sound of the bell, the practitioner or the whole group stands up.)

SECOND EARTH TOUCHING

Touching the earth, I connect with all people and all species
that are alive in this moment in the world with me.

(With the sound of the bell, the practitioner or the whole
group touches the earth.)

I am one with the wonderful pattern of life that radiates out in all directions. I see the close connection between myself and all people and all species, how we share happiness and suffering. I am a great being who has transcended birth and death. I can look at all phenomena such as birth and death, happiness and suffering, with a calm gaze. I am one of those wise spiritual friends—who can be found a little bit everywhere—who radiate peace, understanding, and love, who can touch the nourishing and healing wonders of life, who can embrace the whole world with a loving heart and arms of caring action. I am someone who has enough peace, happiness, and freedom to be able to offer non-fear and the joy of being alive to everyone around me. I do not feel alone or cut off from others. I feel supported by the compassion and joy of great beings, who help me not to drown in despair but to live my life fully, with meaning, peace, and joy. I see myself in each one of you and I see you all in me.

(three breaths)

I am someone who was born disabled or who has become disabled because of war, accident, or illness. I am someone who is caught in a situation of war, oppression, or imprisonment. I am someone who has never enjoyed happiness and peace in family life. Cut off from my roots, I am hungry for understanding and love, and am always looking for beauty, truth, and goodness, which can give meaning to my life and in which I can take refuge.

(three breaths)

I am someone who is at the point of death, and I am very afraid because I do not know what will become of me. I am a child living in a place where there is miserable poverty and disease; my arms and legs are as thin as matchsticks, and I have no future. I am also a manufacturer of armaments that are sold to poor countries. I am the frog swimming in the pond, but I am also the grass snake who needs to feed on the frog. I am the caterpillar and the ant, and also the bird hunting for insects to eat. I am the forest that is being cut down, the rivers and the air that are being polluted. I am also the person who clear-cuts the forest and pollutes the river and the air. I see myself in all species, and I see all species in me.

(Three breaths, then with the sound of the bell, the practitioner or the whole group stands up.)

THIRD EARTH TOUCHING

Touching the earth, I let go of all ideas that I am this body and this limited life span.

(With the sound of the bell, the practitioner or the whole group touches the earth.)

I know that this body, made of the four elements (earth, water, air, fire), is not truly me. I am not limited by this body. I am a river of life of spiritual and blood ancestors, which since beginningless time has flowed to the present and will continue to stream onward into the future without end. I am both my ancestors and my descendants. I am life manifesting in thousands of forms. I inter-am with all people and all species, whether they are peaceful and fearless or suffering and afraid. In this moment, I am present everywhere on this planet. I am also present in the past and in the future. The disintegration of this body does not touch me, just as the falling plum blossoms do not mean the end of the plum tree. I see myself as a wave on the surface of the ocean. My true nature is the ocean water. I see myself in all the other waves, and I see all the other waves in me. The appearance or disappearance of the form of the wave does not affect the ocean.

My Dharma body and spiritual life are not subject to birth and death. I see myself present before the manifestation of this body and after its decomposition. Even in this moment, I see how I exist elsewhere than in this body. My life span is not limited to eighty or ninety years. My life span, just like the life span of a leaf or the buddhas, is unlimited. I can go beyond the idea that I am a body separate in space and time from all other manifestations of life.

(Three breaths, then with the sound of the bell, the practitioner or the whole group stands up.)

EXPLANATION

We suffer because we are caught by the notions of me, the other, life span, etc. The Three Earth Touchings help us to transcend all these notions. They can be represented by a cross and a circle.

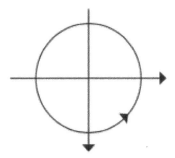

We start with a vertical line, then a horizontal line, and finally a circle. Practicing the first Earth Touching, we visualize our ancestors and our descendants. We prostrate ourselves face-down onto the earth, with our four limbs and forehead touching the ground. The closer our body can be in contact with the earth, the better. In this position, we start to relax all the muscles of our body. We let go of everything we consider to be "me" or "mine" so that we can become one with the stream of life of our ancestors, our own stream of life: "I have spiritual ancestors . . ."

Similarly, for my blood family: "Among my ancestors, . . ."

When we touch the earth like this, we can more easily reconcile with our ancestors. If we are angry with our father, our mother, our teacher, our brother, or our sister, this Earth Touching will help us to reconcile with them. Our father, mother, uncles, aunts, brothers, and sisters, they are all our ancestors. Each one born before us is our ancestor. It is similar for the monastic "family."

Each monastic who received ordination before us is our elder brother or elder sister, even if he or she is younger in biological age than you. Even though you might think they are less knowledgeable than you, or you consider that they practice less well, he or she is still your elder sibling. We respect him as our elder brother; we respect her as our elder sister. We cannot say: "He is no better than me, she does not practice as well as me, so why should I respect him as my elder brother or her as my elder sister?"

We can cultivate the same attitude toward our ancestors. Some had many talents, and some were unskillful. Nevertheless, they are our ancestors, and we have to accept them all. Our parents, our brothers and sisters, all have certain good qualities as well as some shortcomings. The same is true for ourselves. Therefore we accept them as they are. We cannot say: "He is not worthy of being my elder brother. She is not worthy of being my elder sister. What makes them better than me so that they get to be my elder siblings?" Our ancestors are simply ancestors. Whether they are skillful or unskillful, they are still our ancestors. Our parents are simply parents. Whether they were good or unsatisfactory parents, they are still our parents.

In the Buddhist tradition, when someone makes the vow to become a monk or a nun, he or she is seen as the elder son or elder daughter of the Buddha, because he or she has had to leave everything behind, including their family, in order to join the monastic sangha and to take on the role of elder brother or elder sister. For this reason, even though he or she may still be young in age, not wise and not yet able to practice the precepts and Mindful Manners very well, we respect him as our elder brother, we respect her as our elder sister.

When we think, "These monks and nuns are younger than me, they have less understanding of the Dharma than I, they practice less well; why do I have to wait for them, sit lower down the line than them and give them my respect?" When we think like that, we do not understand what *are* our ancestors, what *are* monks, nuns, elder sons, and elder daughters of the Buddha. Even though they make mistakes and sometimes infringe on the precepts, they are still our elder siblings. They are the elder sons and elder daughters of the Buddha. Perhaps we think we can do better than them, but we cannot deny the fact that they are our teacher, our uncle monk, our aunty nun, our elder brother, or our elder sister. Maybe the reason they do not practice so well is because the conditions are not yet sufficient.

We can bring the same approach to our younger brothers and sisters, and to our children. Practicing the first Earth Touching can be particularly helpful when we are jealous of our younger siblings, when we are angry with them or find them hard to accept, when we see them as stubborn, impolite, or difficult. The practice can also help when we are angry with our children, when we dislike them and want to reject them. "Dear Buddha, within me I have strengths, but I also have shortcomings. I know that I still have ups and downs, internal knots, and that I suffer. So why can't I accept my younger siblings and my children with *their* shortcomings? Understanding myself, I can accept everyone." Practicing this Earth Touching, we can reconcile with our ancestors and our descendants. Our parents gave birth to us; they accepted us as their children. In the same way, we can accept them as our parents, we can accept our elder brothers, our elder sisters, our younger siblings. Let us accept all of them, even if they are corrupt or stubborn, even if they have difficulties and are suffering, because we also have similar difficulties. Who are we to reject our parents, our brothers and sisters?

Our teacher has given birth to our spiritual life, and he has accepted us as his students. So why can't we accept our sisters and brothers in the Dharma? Even if they have shortcomings, their ups and downs, and they make mistakes, they are still our elder brothers and sisters and younger brothers and sisters in the Dharma. Our acceptance and reconciliation is the only path that can help them. It is important to practice the first Earth Touching every day, with all our heart, especially when we have difficulties with our parents, our teachers, our siblings.

During the second Earth Touching, we get in contact with all people and all beings alive in the present moment. As in the first exercise, we contemplate the text while prostrating with our four limbs and forehead on the earth. We can turn to the bodhisattvas, great beings alive in the world in this moment. Whether we call them "bodhisattvas" or not, they *are* bodhisattvas because they have solidity, freedom, and love. They are a little bit everywhere, for example, in humanitarian organizations like Doctors Without Borders or Schools Without Borders. There are so many people everywhere in the world working to relieve suffering thanks to their love, solidity, and freedom. Amongst those engaged in humanitarian work, some have solidity, freedom, peace, and happiness. Thanks to these qualities, they do not drown in the ocean of suffering that they face daily. Without their peace, happiness, solidity, and freedom, they would drown in anger and hatred, along with all those they are trying to help. They would be of no help at all.

Around us, wonderful bodhisattvas really exist. We just have to open our eyes to see them and we can join with them: "I am one with you. I take refuge in you and feel nourished by your freedom, your solidity, your peace and happiness." We can connect with them, take refuge in them, to become stronger. You do not have to look far. They are very close; in fact, right here. These great beings are not necessarily elders. Sometimes they are still very young, but we can already recognize in them the solidity, freedom, peace, and happiness that we need.

While practicing this second Earth Touching, we visualize ourselves connecting with them to receive their energy. We feel gratitude for their presence.

Now that we have touched the energy of bodhisattvas, we can get in contact with beings who are still drowning in the ocean of suffering: the victims of wars in the Middle East, hungry children in the developing world, prisoners, people who are suffering, oppressed, and exploited, children who did not have the chance to go to school and instead have to search for scraps of food thrown out with the rubbish . . . They are all us. We are the frog who swims freely in the autumn pond, but we are also the snake who is hunting prey and swallows the frog. The snake needs food to survive as well. This kind of suffering is part of life. Getting in contact with all beings, we touch their suffering and we see ourselves become one with them. However, we do not drown in the ocean of suffering, because we have a place of refuge. The bodhisattvas and great beings are our refuge. We do not have to look far for people living in freedom, peace, and happiness. They are present in our sangha. Neither do we have to look far for those who suffer. They are also in our sangha. We are one with them. As soon as we recognize this, even our facial expressions as we look at them will already communicate that we understand their suffering. If we can love them, they will feel it immediately. The second Earth Touching brings us happiness, as we are practicing. It helps us to recognize the people who have freedom, solidity, and compassion, so that we can take refuge in them and become one with them. This Earth Touching also helps us to recognize those who suffer because of their wrong perceptions, internal knots, and past misfortunes, so that we can take them in our arms, understand them, and become one with them. When we take action, we do so having looked deeply and from a place of compassion. Where does this compassion come from? It comes from our looking deeply and understanding.

In this Earth Touching, we take refuge in beings who are healthy, who live in peace and freedom with solidity and happiness, and we become one with them. At the same time, we become one with beings who have difficulties and who suffer. This communion helps us to allow compassion to be born. As soon as love has been generated, it manifests in our eyes, our hands, and our feet, and we are already helping others. When we help others, we are also helping ourselves. The compassion born in our hearts brings happiness to us even before we extend our help. We do not know if our love has brought happiness to others yet, but we will already feel the benefit of the compassionate nectar in us. We have learned that without love in our hearts, we suffer, and the greater the compassion we can give rise to, the more extensive the happiness that results.

The third Earth Touching encompasses time and space. "Touching the earth, I abandon the idea that I am only this body." This practice was taught by the Zen master Tang Hoi. Habitually, we think that we are only this body. In France, a group of women have been protesting for their right to choose abortion. Concurrently, another group of women organized a protest march against the first group. Those who support the right to choose defend their view in this way: this body is mine; I must have the right to do what I like with my body. Many people think they are right. But according to Buddhist wisdom, this view is not quite right: our body is not only ours; it also belongs to our ancestors, our parents, our descendants, to humanity and the whole cosmos. Let us look deeply. The peace and joy of my body are linked to the peace and joy of other bodies.

In the third Earth Touching, we see that we are not only this body, which was born on a certain day of a certain month in a certain year. The Buddha has reminded us of this truth many times in numerous sutras: this body is not me. When we practice correctly the first Earth Touching, we can already see this truth: our ancestors are us; our parents, our brothers, our sisters, and our children are us. We are so much more than we think we are. In this Earth Touching, we unite ourselves with the whole stream of life. What I consider to be "me" transcends the limits of this physical body.

The first Earth Touching already contains the third: "Touching the earth, I let go of the idea that this body is all that I have." I train myself to abandon the belief that this body is me, and that I am only this body. I practice to understand that my life span is not limited to eighty or ninety years. I can see my existence before the manifestation of this body and after its decomposition. My life span is un-limited. This is the third Touching of the Earth. We see that insight from the third exercise comes from practicing the first and second. We think that the third Earth Touching is more difficult to practice than the first two, but effectively, if we have succeeded in practicing the first two, we have already practiced the third.

Practicing deeply these Earth Touchings every day, we can liberate ourselves from birth and death.

THIRD EXERCISE
Touching the Three Jewels

(While a sangha member reads the gatha [if you are alone, you can read it yourself], you breathe in on the first, third, fifth, and seventh lines, and breathe out on the other lines. At the end, bend forward to touch the earth in the prostrate position. Remain in this position for as long as you wish, following your breathing and keeping the words of the gatha alive in your mind. You do not need to memorize all the lines if it prevents you from concentrating on their meaning. Retaining one or two lines can be enough for your meditation.)

> *With all my heart,*
> *Sincerely, I take refuge*
> *In the Buddha, the Dharma, and the sangha*
> *Present in the ten directions*
> *As well as in myself,*
> *Present in all realms of all things,*
> *Transcending the past, the present, and the future,*
> *Touching the earth, I surrender myself entirely.*

EXPLANATION

The first time we heard this gatha in Plum Village, it was pouring with rain. Just before practicing, we had been sitting facing the big picture windows in the meditation hall, watching the rain falling on the earth.

This gatha can help you meditate while you touch the earth. Just like drops of rain, we also touch the earth. Each of us is like a raindrop, and our earth needs the rain.

The ten directions are the eight directions of the compass plus the zenith and the nadir. We say that they all contain the Buddha because the Buddha is the awakened part of our being, which can manifest anywhere. We do not have to go to Bodhgaya in India to find the Buddha.

The Dharma is the teachings on things as they are. If we are awake in the present moment, everything around us can be a source of teaching: a flower, a rock, even an insult.

The sangha is the combination of human and non-human elements that support us in our practice. The soft grass we are sitting on, as well as the friends whom we are sitting with, all are a part of our sangha.

In the same way, each cell of our bodies contains the Buddha, the Dharma, and the sangha. Whether we habitually regard this or that part of our body as clean or unclean, they are all the Buddha, the Dharma, and the sangha. Every cell of our body contains the element earth. When we touch the earth, we could not possibly be nearer to her. We are not different from the earth we touch.

While prostrating, maybe you will feel an intense joy and tears will flow, feeling as if perfumed flowers are all around you, washed by the rain. Even if the earth seems inanimate, she contains the seeds that will become flowers. When you die, as you have already died thousands of times, a flower will bloom to welcome you home. Touching the earth is to die: dying *and* touching happiness. Those who wish to die and forever leave behind the red dust of this earth, you do not have to wait for death to call. You can already surrender and let go in the here and now.

The realm of Dharma refers to the objects of our mind. Anything can be an object of our mind, and therefore is included within the realm of Dharma. The realm of Dharma is something miraculous because, even though it is a part of the phenomenal world, it expresses the ultimate nature of things. Everything that we can conceive of contains the Buddha, the Dharma, and the sangha.

We have the possibility to transcend the past, the present, and the future. The Buddha does not only belong to the past, to the fifth and sixth centuries before the Common Era. The Buddha can be here, with us right now, when we know how to be mindful. What were you before being born as a human being? Were you a cloud? The Buddha was in that cloud. Perhaps you were a mosquito; the Buddha was also in that mosquito.

What will you be in the future? Will you be a drop of rain? The Buddha, the Dharma, and the sangha will be in that raindrop. Do not think that we have the possibility of meeting the Buddha, Dharma, and sangha only during this lifetime, or that our chance to meet them will be even better in the future.

When we touch the earth, we develop humility as we bow down. We grow because we are making progress in our understanding. Although in reality we are nothing, at the same time we are in harmony with the whole universe.

When you meditate touching the earth, it is important to feel at ease. You surrender and simply enjoy your mindful breathing. In this position, it is very easy to abandon all your thoughts and give up all ideas about yourself. Let go completely, holding on to nothing. This means that not a trace of pride will be left. You will stop judging yourself as either stupid or intelligent, worthy or unworthy. Pride is a burden that we can put down when we touch the earth.

APPENDIX

CEREMONY FOR RECITING
THE FIVE MINDFULNESS TRAININGS

1. Sitting Meditation (12 Minutes)

2. Opening Verse

> The Dharma is deep and lovely.
> We now have a chance to see, study, and practice it.
> We vow to realize its true meaning.

[BELL]

3. The Insight That Brings Us to the Other Shore

Avalokiteshvara, while practicing deeply with the Insight that Brings Us to the Other Shore, suddenly discovered that all of the five skandhas are equally empty, and with this realization he overcame all ill-being.

Listen, Sariputra, this body itself is emptiness, and emptiness itself is this body. This body is not other than emptiness, and emptiness is not other than this body. The same is true of feelings, perceptions, mental formations, and consciousness.

Listen, Sariputra, all phenomena bear the mark of emptiness; their true nature is the nature of no birth, no death, no being, no non-being, no defilement, no purity, no increasing, no decreasing.

That is why in emptiness, body, feelings, perceptions, mental formations, and consciousness are not separate self-entities.

The eighteen realms of phenomena, which are the six sense organs, six sense objects, and the six consciousnesses, are also not separate self-entities.

The twelve links of interdependent arising and their extinction are also not separate self entities.

Ill-being, the causes of ill-being, the end of ill-being, the path, insight and attainment, are also not separate self-entities. Whoever can see this no longer needs anything to attain.

Bodhisattvas who practice the Insight That Brings Us to the Other Shore see no more obstacles in their mind, and because there are no more obstacles in their mind, they can overcome all fear, destroy all wrong perceptions, and realize perfect nirvana.

All buddhas in the past, present, and future, by practicing the Insight That Brings Us to the Other Shore, are all capable of attaining authentic and perfect enlightenment.

Therefore, Sariputra, it should be known that the Insight That Brings Us to the Other Shore is a great mantra, the most illuminating mantra, the highest mantra, a mantra beyond compare, the true wisdom that has the power to put an end to all kinds of suffering.

Therefore let us proclaim a mantra to praise the Insight That Brings Us to the Other Shore.

Gate, Gate, Paragate, Parasamgate, Bodhi Svaha!

[BELL, BELL, BELL]

4. Sanghakarman Procedure

Sanghakarman Master: Has the entire community assembled?

Sangha Convener: The entire community has assembled.

Sanghakarman Master: Is there harmony in the community?

Sangha Convener: Yes, there is harmony.

Sanghakarman Master: Is there anyone not able to be present

who has asked to be represented, and have they declared themselves to have done their best to study and practice the Five Mindfulness Trainings?

Sangha Convener: No, there is not.

or

Sangha Convener: Yes, [NAME], for health reasons, cannot be at the recitation today. She has asked [NAME] to represent her, and she declares that she has done her best to study and practice the mindfulness trainings.

Sanghakarman Master: What is the reason for the community gathering today?

Sangha Convener: The community has gathered to practice the recitation of the Five Mindfulness Trainings.

Sanghakarman Master: Noble community, please listen. Today, [DATE], has been declared to be the Mindfulness Training Recitation Day. We have gathered at the appointed time. The noble community is ready to hear and recite the mindfulness trainings in an atmosphere of harmony, and the recitation can proceed. Is this statement clear and complete?

Everyone: Clear and complete.

[BELL]

5. Introductory Words

Dear Sangha, this is the moment when we enjoy reciting the Five Mindfulness Trainings together. The Five Mindfulness Trainings represent the Buddhist vision for a global spirituality and ethic. They are a concrete expression of the Buddha's teachings on the Four Noble Truths and the Noble Eightfold Path, the path of right understanding and true love, leading to healing, transformation, and happiness for ourselves and for the world. To practice the Five Mindfulness Trainings is to cultivate the insight of interbeing, or Right

View, which can remove all discrimination, intolerance, anger, fear, and despair. If we live according to the Five Mindfulness Trainings, we are already on the path of a bodhisattva. Knowing we are on that path, we are not lost in confusion about our life in the present or in fears about the future.

Please listen to each mindfulness training with a serene mind, breathe mindfully, and answer yes silently, every time you see that you have made an effort to study, practice, and observe the mindfulness training read.

6. Reciting the Five Mindfulness Trainings

THE FIRST MINDFULNESS TRAINING:
REVERENCE FOR LIFE

Aware of the suffering caused by the destruction of life, I am committed to cultivating the insight of interbeing and compassion, and learning ways to protect the lives of people, animals, plants, and minerals. I am determined not to kill, not to let others kill, and not to support any act of killing in the world, in my thinking, or in my way of life. Seeing that harmful actions arise from anger, fear, greed, and intolerance, which in turn come from dualistic and discriminative thinking, I will cultivate openness, nondiscrimination, and nonattachment to views in order to transform violence, fanaticism, and dogmatism in myself and in the world.

This is the first of the Five Mindfulness Trainings. Have you made an effort to study, practice, and observe it during the past two weeks?

[THREE BREATHS]

[BELL][1]

---

1. After three breaths, the bell master "stops" the bell by holding the striker gently against the rim, thereby signaling the reader to continue with the next mindfulness training.

THE SECOND MINDFULNESS TRAINING:
TRUE HAPPINESS

Aware of the suffering caused by exploitation, social injustice, stealing, and oppression, I am committed to practicing generosity in my thinking, speaking, and acting. I am determined not to steal and not to possess anything that should belong to others. I will share my time, energy, and material resources with those who are in need. I will practice looking deeply to see that the happiness and suffering of others are not separate from my own happiness and suffering; that true happiness is not possible without understanding and compassion; and that running after wealth, fame, power, and sensual pleasures can bring much suffering and despair. I am aware that happiness depends on my mental attitude and not on external conditions, and that I can live happily in the present moment simply by remembering that I already have more than enough conditions to be happy. I am committed to practicing Right Livelihood so that I can help reduce the suffering of living beings on Earth and stop contributing to climate change.

This is the second of the Five Mindfulness Trainings. Have you made an effort to study, practice, and observe it during the past two weeks?

[THREE BREATHS]

[BELL]

THE THIRD MINDFULNESS TRAINING: TRUE LOVE

Aware of the suffering caused by sexual misconduct, I am committed to cultivating responsibility and learning ways to protect the safety and integrity of individuals, couples, families, and society. Knowing that sexual desire is not love, and that sexual activity motivated by craving always harms myself as well as others, I am determined not to engage in sexual relations without true love and a deep, long-term commitment made known to my family and friends. I will do everything in my power to protect children from sexual abuse, and to prevent couples and families from being broken by sexual misconduct. Seeing that body and mind are not separate, I am committed to learning appropriate ways to take care of my sexual energy and cultivating loving-kindness, compassion, joy, and inclusiveness—which are the four basic elements of true love—for my greater happiness and the greater happiness of others. Practicing true love, we know that we will continue beautifully into the future.

This is the third of the Five Mindfulness Trainings. Have you made an effort to study, practice, and observe it during the past two weeks?

[THREE BREATHS]

[BELL]

THE FOURTH MINDFULNESS TRAINING: LOVING SPEECH AND DEEP LISTENING

Aware of the suffering caused by unmindful speech and the inability to listen to others, I am committed to cultivating loving speech and compassionate listening in order to relieve suffering and to promote reconciliation and peace in myself and among other people, ethnic and religious groups, and nations. Knowing that words can create happiness or suffering, I am committed to speaking truthfully, using words that inspire confidence, joy, and hope. When anger is manifesting in me, I am determined not to speak. I will practice mindful breathing and walking in order to recognize and to look deeply into my anger. I know that the roots of anger can be found in my wrong perceptions and lack of understanding of the suffering in myself and in the other person. I will speak and listen in a way that can help myself and the other person to transform suffering and see the way out of difficult situations. I am determined not to spread news that I do not know to be certain and not to utter words that can cause division or discord. I will practice Right Diligence to nourish my capacity for understanding, love, joy, and inclusiveness, and gradually transform anger, violence, and fear that lie deep in my consciousness.

This is the fourth of the Five Mindfulness Trainings. Have you made an effort to study, practice, and observe it during the past two weeks?

[THREE BREATHS]

[BELL]

THE FIFTH MINDFULNESS TRAINING: NOURISHMENT AND HEALING

Aware of the suffering caused by unmindful consumption, I am committed to cultivating good health, both physical and mental, for myself, my family, and my society, by practicing mindful eating, drinking, and consuming. I will practice looking deeply into how I consume the Four Kinds of Nutriments, namely edible foods, sense impressions, volition, and consciousness. I am determined not to gamble, or to use alcohol, drugs, or any other products that contain toxins, such as certain websites, electronic games, music, TV programs, films, magazines, books, and conversations. I will practice coming back to the present moment to be in touch with the refreshing, healing, and nourishing elements in me and around me, not letting regrets and sorrow drag me back into the past, nor letting anxieties, fear, or craving pull me out of the present moment. I am determined not to try to cover up loneliness, anxiety, or other suffering by losing myself in consumption. I will contemplate interbeing and consume in a way that preserves peace, joy, and well-being in my body and consciousness, and in the collective body and consciousness of my family, my society, and the Earth.

This is the fifth of the Five Mindfulness Trainings. Have you made an effort to study, practice, and observe it during the past two weeks?

[THREE BREATHS]

[BELL]

7. Concluding Words

Dear Sangha, we have recited the Five Mindfulness Trainings, the foundation of happiness for the individual, the family, and society. We should recite them regularly so that our study and practice of the mindfulness trainings can deepen day by day.

[BELL X 2]

> *Reciting the trainings, practicing the way of awareness*
> *gives rise to benefits without limit.*
> *We vow to share the fruits with all beings.*
> *We vow to offer tribute to parents, teachers, friends,*
> *and numerous beings*
> *who give guidance and support along the path.*

[BELL, BELL, BELL]

RESOURCES

PLUM VILLAGE

*Connect with Thich Nhat Hanh's
international community*

For news, online retreats, and
live mindfulness sessions, visit
plumvillage.org

Download the Plum Village app for free
meditations and relaxations:
plumvillage.app

THICH NHAT HANH FOUNDATION

Planting seeds of compassion

The Thich Nhat Hanh Foundation is the charitable
foundation dedicated to continuing the teachings and
legacy of Zen master Thich Nhat Hanh. By becoming
a supporter, you join many others who want to learn
and share his life-changing practices of mindfulness
and engaged Buddhism, and bring change to ourselves,
our society, and our planet. To find out how you
can help support his legacy, and to subscribe to
our community newsletter, visit tnhf.org.

Immerse yourself in mindfulness on a residential retreat at one of Thich Nhat Hanh's mindfulness practice centers in the US:

Deer Park Monastery, Escondido, CA: deerparkmonastery.org

Magnolia Grove Monastery, Batesville, MS:
magnoliagrovemonastery.org

Blue Cliff Monastery, Pine Bush, NY: bluecliffmonastery.org

To find out more about centers in Europe and Asia,
visit plumvillage.org.

Discover international networks of Engaged Buddhism in Thich Nhat Hanh's tradition:

EARTH HOLDERS	ARISE
A Mindful Earth Justice Initiative	*Awakening through Race, Intersectionality, and Social Equity*
earthholder.training	arisesangha.org

THE WAKE UP MOVEMENT	WAKE UP SCHOOLS
Young Buddhists and Non-Buddhists for a Healthy and Compassionate Society	*Cultivating Mindfulness in Education*
wkup.org	wakeupschools.org

Facebook: thichnhathanh | Instagram: thichnhathanhsangha
Twitter: @thichnhathanh | URL: plumvillage.org
URL: thichnhathanhfoundation.org